INSTRUCTIONS

FROM THE

REGENTS OF THE UNIVERSITY,

TO THE SEVERAL

COLLEGES, ACADEMIES,

AND

Other Literary Institutions subject to their Visitation,

PRESCRIBING THE REQUISITES AND FORMS FOR

REPORTS, APPLICATIONS, &c.

REVISED EDITION.

PREPARED IN OBEDIENCE TO AN ORDER OF THE REGENTS, OCTOBER 20, 1853.

ALBANY:
PRINTED BY C. VAN BENTHUYSEN.

1853.

MEMORANDUM.

As the edition of the "Instructions" published in 1849 is exhausted, the Regents, some time since, directed the preparation of another. The reader will find in it all the Laws, relating to Colleges and Academies, that have been passed subsequent to the above year.

Occasion has also been taken to revise and consolidate the Ordinances of the Board, and several important changes and additions have been introduced relative to the Annual Report of Academies. The standard of age has been raised, and the requisites of classical students and those in the higher branches of English education have been somewhat increased.

This Ordinance, with its additions and amendments, will be found at page 59, and extends to page 65. The Annual reports of Academies, to be made in 1855, must be in conformity to it. But it will be observed that the ordinance does not come in force until May 1, 1854, and reports referring to a period previous to this, may be in conformity to the "Instructions" of 1849.

Two copies of this edition of the Instructions will be sent to every College and Academy subject to the visitation of the Regents; one for the use of its President or principal and other teachers, and to be preserved in its library; and the other for the use of its trustees, in making out their Annual report, and to be kept by their Secretary or Treasurer, having charge of their books and papers.

REGENTS OF THE UNIVERSITY, DECEMBER, 1853.

HORATIO SEYMOUR, Governor, ex-officio.
SANFORD E. CHURCH, Lt. Governor, ex-officio.
HENRY S. RANDALL, Secretary of State, ex-officio.

1825, Jan. 12. JOHN GREIG.
1826, Jan. 26. GULIAN C. VERPLANCK, LL.D.
1829, March 31. GERRIT Y. LANSING.
1829, March 31. JOHN K. PAIGE.
1833, Feb. 5. ERASTUS CORNING.
1833, April 4. PROSPER M. WETMORE.
1834, April 17. JOHN L. GRAHAM.
1835, April 8. JOHN McLEAN.
1842, Feb. 1. GIDEON HAWLEY, LL.D.
1842, March 24. DAVID BUEL.
1844. May 4. JAMES S. WADSWORTH.
1844, May 4. JOHN V. L. PRUYN, LL.D.
1845, May 10. JABEZ D. HAMMOND, LL.D.
1846, Feb. 2. JOHN L. O'SULLIVAN.
1846, Feb. 2. ROBERT CAMPBELL.
1847, May 6. Rev. SAMUEL LUCKEY, D.D.
1847, Sept. 22. ROBERT G. RANKIN.
1849, Feb. 6. PHILIP S. VAN RENSSELAER.
1851, March 18. Rev. JOHN N. CAMPBELL, D.D.

OFFICERS OF THE BOARD.

GERRIT Y. LANSING, *Chancellor.*
JOHN GREIG, *Vice-Chancellor.*
T. ROMEYN BECK, *Secretary.*

MEETINGS OF THE REGENTS.

The first or annual meeting is according to law, held on the evening of the second Thursday in January, at the Senate Chamber in the Capitol.

The meetings continue to be held during the session of the Legislature, and as often as the nature of the business before the Board demands. They are adjourned from week to week.

It is, therefore, recommended to Academies to make all their communications in due season. Applications for money to purchase books and apparatus should be sent in before the middle of February, and for all other purposes, before the middle of March. The Board usually adjourns about the 10th of April.

Special meetings can only be held, after ten days' notice has been given of the same in the State Paper. They are but seldom called, except for the considera-tion of matters referred to the Regents by the Legislature. There is, how-ever, a standing order requiring a special meeting to be held on some day in October of each year.

CONTENTS.

SELECT SCHOOLS.

COLLEGES.

APPENDIX.

INSTRUCTIONS, &c.

I. Revised Statutes of the State of New-York, relative to Public Instruction in Colleges, Academies, and Select Schools.

(From the third edition, published in 1846.)

CHAP. XV., TITLE I.

OF THE UNIVERSITY OF THIS STATE, AND OF THE FOUNDATION AND GOVERNMENT OF COLLEGES, ACADEMIES, AND SELECT SCHOOLS.

ARTICLE FIRST.

Of the organization and powers of the board of regents.

SEC. 1. University instituted; government vested in regents.
2. Name and corporate powers.
3. Number of regents; who members ex officio.
4. How appointed; how removed.
5. Vacancies; how supplied.
6. Officers; who; how chosen; tenure of office.
7. Who to preside; president has casting vote.
8. To be an annual meeting; time and place.
9. Place of other meetings; by whom appointed.
10. Number of regents a quorum; power to adjourn.*
11. How meetings ordered and called.
12. Treasurer to keep account of monies received and paid.
13. Secretary to keep journal.
14. Regents may have access to, and take copies of papers,
15 Must visit colleges and academies, and report annually.
16. May make by-laws.
17. Grants must be applied to uses for which made.
18. Regents may confer degrees.
19. Their degree of M. D. to give authority to practice physic.
20. May grant certain honorary degrees.
21. May in certain cases supply vacancies in offices of president and principal.
22 & 23. Tenure of office of such person; powers, emoluments, &c.
24. Regents have control of income of literature fund; application thereof.†
25 & 26. How distribution thereof to be regulated.
27. 12,000 dollars of income to be annually divided.
28 to 30. Excess applied in purchase of books, educating teachers, &c.

* See note to section 10. † See note to section 24.

31. Institutions having departments for teaching to report annually to superintendent of common schools.
32. 28,000 dollars added to literature fund; condition of its distribution.
33. Academies receiving certain sum to keep department for common school teachers.
34 & 35. Regents annually to deliver schedule of dividends to comptroller, who is to pay them to each institution, &c.
36. Regents must require annual returns from seminaries.
37. How return to be attested; what it must contain.
38. Regents must report annually to the legislature an abstract of returns.
39. Regents to prescribe forms of returns.
40. Their necessary expenses to be paid out of treasury.
41. And to be audited by the comptroller.
42. Regents to have power to send for persons and papers.
43. Exemption of regents in New-York from attendance repealed.

SECTION 1. An university is instituted in this state, of which the government is, and shall continue to be, vested in a board of regents.

§ 2. This university is incorporated under, and is and shall be known by, the name of "The Regents of the University of the State of New-York;" and by that name shall have perpetual succession, power to sue and be sued, and to make and use a common seal and alter the same at pleasure, to hold property real and personal to the amount of the annual income of forty thousand bushels of wheat, and to buy and sell and otherwise dispose of, lands and chattels.

§ 3. The regents are twenty-two in number, including the governor, lieutenant-governor and secretary of state, who are members of the board by virtue of their offices. [*Sec.* 2, *of chap.* 142 *of* 1842.]

§ 4. With the exception of the governor and lieutenant-governor,* the regents are appointed by the legislature, and may be removed by a concurrent resolution of the senate and assembly.

§ 5. All vacancies happening in the offices of those so appointed, shall be supplied by the legislature, in the manner in which the state officers are directed to be appointed, in the fifth chapter of this act.

§ 6. The officers of this corporation are a chancellor, a vice-chancellor, a treasurer,† and a secretary, all of whom are chosen by the regents, by ballot, a plurality of votes being sufficient to a choice. They hold their respective offices during the pleasure of the board.

§ 7. The chancellor, and if he shall be absent, the vice-chancellor, and if both be absent, the senior regent in the order of appointment, shall preside at all meetings of the regents, and have a casting vote in case of a division.

§ 8. There shall be an annual meeting of the regents on the evening of the second Thursday in January, in every year, at the senate chamber in the capitol.

§ 9. All meetings, except adjourned meetings, shall be held at such time and place as the chancellor, or in case his office be

* "And Secretary of State" should be here inserted on a revision.

† By an act passed January 25, 1832, the Literature Fund, and the United States Deposit Fund, so far as the same is now granted to academies, were placed under the control of the Comptroller of the State, and so far the office of treasurer is abolished; but other appropriations are usually made payable to the Regents, and the Secretary is for this purpose declared *ex officio* treasurer.

vacant, or he be absent from the state, the vice-chancellor, or if he be also absent, or the offices of both be vacant, the senior regent in the state, shall appoint.

§ 10. Eight regents attending, shall be a board for the transaction of business; and the regents present, whether a quorum or otherwise, shall have power to adjourn from time to time, not exceeding ten days at a time.*

§ 11. A meeting shall be ordered and called by the officer authorized to appoint the same, as often as three regents, in writing, so request; and the order shall be published in the state paper at least ten days prior to the meeting.

§ 12. The treasurer shall keep an account of all monies by him received and paid out.

§ 13. The secretary shall keep a journal of the proceedings of the regents, in which the ayes and noes on all questions shall be entered, if requested by any one of the regents present.

§ 14. Each regent may always have access to, and be permitted to take copies of, all the books and papers of the corporation.

§ 15. The regents are authorized and required, by themselves or their committees, to visit and inspect all the colleges and academies in this state, examine into the condition and system of education and discipline therein, and make an annual report of the same to the legislature.

§ 16. The regents shall have power to make such by-laws and ordinances as they shall judge most expedient for the accomplishment of the trust reposed in them.

§ 17. Grants made to the regents for certain uses and purposes shall not be applied, either wholly or in part, to any other uses.

§ 18. The regents shall have the right of conferring by diploma under their common seal, on any person whom they may judge worthy thereof, such degrees above that of master of arts, as are known to, and usually granted by, any college or University in Europe.

§ 19. A degree of doctor of medicine, granted by the regents, shall authorize the person on whom it is conferred, to practice physic and surgery within this state.

§ 20. The regents of the university may in their discretion confer the honorary degree of doctor of medicine upon such persons, not to exceed four in any one year, as may be recommended to them for that purpose, by the medical society of this state, but such honorary degree shall in no case be a license to practice physic or surgery. [*Chap.* 366 *of* 1840.]

§ 21. In case the trustees of any college shall leave the office of president of the college, or the trustees of any academy shall leave the office of principal of the academy, vacant, for the space of one year, the regents shall fill up such vacancy, unless a reasonable cause shall be assigned for such delay, to their satisfaction.

* "Six members of the Board of Regents shall hereafter be necessary to form a quorum for the transaction of business." [Sec. 4 of Chap. 184 of the Laws of 1853.]

§ 22. The person so appointed, shall continue in office during the pleasure of the regents, and shall have the same powers, and the same salary, emoluments and privileges, as his next immediate predecessor in office enjoyed.

§ 23. If such president or principal had no immediate predecessor in office, he shall have such salary as the regents shall direct, to be paid by the trustees out of the funds or property of their college or academy.

§ 24. The regents shall have the control of the whole income arising from the literature fund, and *shall annually divide such income into eight equal parts, and assign one part thereof to each senate district.** They shall annually distribute the part so assigned to each district, among such of the incorporated seminaries of learning, exclusive of colleges within such district, as are now subject, or shall become subject, to their visitation by a valid corporate act.

§ 25. Every such distribution shall be made in proportion to the number of pupils in each seminary, who for four months during the preceding year, shall have pursued therein, classical studies, or the higher branches of English education, or both.

§ 26. No pupil in any such seminary shall be deemed to have pursued classical studies, unless he shall have advanced at least so far as to have read in Latin the first book of the Æneid; nor to have pursued the higher branches of English education, unless he shall have advanced beyond such knowledge of arithmetic, (including vulgar and decimal fractions,) and of English grammar and geography, as is usually obtained in common schools.

§ 27. There shall be twelve thousand dollars of the revenues of the literature fund, annually distributed by the regents of the university, to the academies and schools which now are or hereafter may be subject to the visitation of the regents, in the manner now provided by law; which monies shall be exclusively appropriated and expended by the trustees of such academies and schools respectively, towards paying the salaries of tutors. [*Sec.* 1 *of chap.* 140 *of* 1834.]

§ 28. Any portion of the excess of the literature fund over the sum of twelve thousand dollars, may, in the discretion of the regents, be assigned to any academy or school subject to their visitation, and subject to such rules and regulations as they may prescribe, for the purchase of new text books, maps and globes, or philosophical or chemical apparatus: such sum shall not exceed two hundred and fifty dollars in any one year. But no part of the said excess shall be actually paid over, unless the trustees of the academy or school to which it is to be appropriated shall raise and apply an equal sum of money to the same object. [*Sec.* 2 *of same chapter.*]

* Sec. 24. The part in italics was repealed by virtue of the enactment contained in sec. 1, chap. 258 of 1847, which required the apportionment to be made among the academies subject to the visitation of the Regents "throughout the State, in proportion to the number of pupils in each, who shall have pursued the requisite studies to entitle them to share in said distribution."

This last enactment continues in force. EDIT.

§ 29. The revenue of the literature fund now in the treasury, and the excess of the annual revenue of said fund hereafter to be paid into the treasury, over the sum of twelve thousand dollars or portions thereof, may be distributed by the regents of the University, if they shall deem expedient, to the academies subject to their visitation, or a portion of them, to be expended as hereinafter mentioned. [*Sec.* 1 *of chap.* 241 *of* 1834.]*

§ 30. The trustees of academies to which any distribution of money shall be made by virtue of this act, shall cause the same to be expended in educating teachers of common schools, in such manner and under such regulations as said regents shall prescribe. [*Sec.* 2 *of same chapter.*]

§ 31. The institutions in which departments for the instruction of common school teachers are or shall be established, shall make to the superintendent of common schools an annual report of the condition of those departments, in such form and containing such information as he may from time to time require; and in respect to the organization and management of the departments and the course of studies therein, the said institutions shall be governed by such direction as he may prescribe; and he may direct the said forms and directions to be printed by the state printer. [*Sec.* 4 *of chap.* 241 *of* 1837.]†

§ 32. The sum of twenty-eight thousand dollars of the income aforesaid shall be annually paid over, on and after the first day of January next, to the literature fund, which, together with the sum of twelve thousand dollars of the present literature fund, shall be annually distributed among the academies in the *several senatorial districts* by the regents of the university, in the *manner now provided by law*;‡ but no academy shall hereafter be allowed to participate in the annual distribution of the literature fund, until the regents of the university shall be satisfied that a proper building has been erected and finished to furnish suitable and necessary accommodation for such school, and that such academy is furnished with a suitable library and philosophical apparatus, and that a proper preceptor has been and is employed for the instruction of the pupils at such academy; and further, that the regents shall, on being satisfied that such building, library and apparatus are sufficient for the purposes intended, and that the whole is of the value at least of twenty-five hundred dollars,§ permit such academy or school to place itself under the visitation of the regents, and thereafter to share in the distribution of the moneys above mentioned, or any other of the literature fund in the manner now provided by law. The regents of the university may also admit to such distribution, and to any other of the literature fund, any incorporated school, or school founded and governed by any literary

* The appropriations in sections 27, 28 and 29 are now (under the constitution of 1846,) made periodically, and depend on the action of the Legislature from time to time.

† Sects 29, 30 and 31 have been modified by subsequent enactments: see Session Laws of 1849, 1851, 1852 and 1853, on common school teaching, as quoted hereafter. EDIT.

‡ See note to sec. 24. § As to the $2,500, see chap. 544 of the Laws of 1851.

corporation other than theological or medical, in which the usual academic studies are pursued, and which shall have been in like manner subjected to their visitation and would in all other respects, were it incorporated as an academy, be entitled to such distribution. [*Sec.* 8 *of chap.* 237 *of* 1838. *U. S. Deposit Fund.*]*

§ 33. It shall be the duty of the regents of the university to require of every academy receiving a distributive share of public money, under the preceding section, equal to seven hundred dollars per annum, to establish and maintain in such academy a department for the instruction of common school teachers, under the direction of the said regents, as a condition of receiving their distributive share of every such academy. [*Sec.* 9 *of same chapter.*]

§ 34. The regents of the university shall annually deliver to the comptroller a schedule of the distribution of the income of the said literature fund, designating the several institutions entitled to a participation, and the amount awarded to each: which schedule shall be delivered immediately after each annual distribution, and shall be authenticated by the signature of the chancellor and secretary of the said regents of the university, and their corporate seal. [*Sec.* 3 *of chap.* 8 *of* 1832.]

§ 35. The comptroller shall draw his warrant on the treasurer, in favor of each institution, for the sum so awarded to it, and shall direct the manner in which the same shall be receipted and drawn from the treasury. [*Sec.* 4 *of same chapter.*]

§ 36. The regents shall require each seminary subject to their visitation, to make an annual return, on or before the first day of February in each year, to the secretary of their board.

§ 37. Every such return shall be attested by the oath either of the principal instructor in the seminary by which it shall be made, or of one of the trustees thereof, and shall contain:

1. The names and ages of all the pupils instructed in such seminary, during the preceding year, and the time that each was so instructed.

2. A particular statement of the studies pursued by each pupil at the commencement of his instruction, and of his subsequent studies, until the date of the report, together with the books such student shall have studied in whole or in part; and if in part what portion.

3. An account or estimate of the cost or value of the library, philosophical and chemical apparatus, and mathematical and other scientific instruments, belonging to the seminary.

4. The names of the instructors employed in the seminary, and the compensation paid to each.

5. An account of the funds, income, debts and incumbrances, of the seminary, and of the application therein of the monies last received from the regents.

* Under the last paragraph of this section, the grammar schools of Columbia college, and of the University of the city of New-York, and more recently, the grammar school of Madison university, have been admitted to share in the Literature Fund.

§ 38. The regents shall, annually, and on or before the first day of March in each year, report to the legislature an abstract of all the returns made to them, embracing a general view of the particulars contained therein; and shall also state in their report the distribution made by them, during the preceding year, of the income of the literature fund, the names of the seminaries sharing in such distribution, and the amount received by each.

§ 39. The regents shall prescribe the forms of all returns, which they shall require from colleges and other seminaries of learning, subject to their visitation; and may direct such forms, and such instructions, as from time to time shall be given by them as visiters, to be printed by the state printer.

§ 40. The expenses of such printing, and all other necessary expenses incurred by the regents, as a board, in the discharge of their official duties, shall be audited by the comptroller and paid out of the treasury.

§ 41. The comptroller shall annually audit and settle the accounts for necessary incidental expenses of the said regents of the university. [*Sec.* 2 *of chap.* 8 *of* 1832.]

§ 42. The regents of the university of the state of New-York, and any committee thereof, in the discharge of any duty required by law, or by resolution of the senate or assembly, may require any proof or information relating thereto, to be verified by oath, and shall for such purposes (and no other) have the powers now by law vested in any committee of either house authorized to send for persons and papers. [*Chap.* 226 *of* 1839.]

§ 43. So much of the act entitled "An act to amend the act entitled 'An act relative to the University,' passed April 17, 1815;" as exempts the regents residing in the city of New-York from attendance at the meetings of the regents to be held during the session of the legislature is hereby repealed.(*a*) [*Sec.* 3 *of chap.* 179 *of* 1845.]

ARTICLE SECOND.

Of the powers and duties of trustees of colleges.

§ 44. The trustees of every college to which a charter shall be granted by the state, shall be a corporation.

(*a*) The act of April 17th, 1815, referred to in this section, is in the following words:

An act to amend the act entitled "An act relative to the University." Passed April 17, 1815. Chap. 207, p. 208.

WHEREAS the regents of the university, in their report to the legislature, have suggested an amendment of the law in respect to their meetings, and the same appearing to be reasonable, Therefore,

§ 1. Be it enacted by the People of the State of New-York, represented in Senate and Assembly, That if any regent (except such as reside in the city of New-York) shall not attend at

§ 45. The trustees shall meet upon their own adjournment, and as often as they shall be summoned by their chairman, or in his absence, by the senior trustee, upon the request in writing of any other three trustees.

§ 46. Notice of the time and place of every such meeting shall be given in a newspaper printed in the county where such college is situate, at least six days before the meeting; and every trustee resident in such county, shall be previously notified in writing, of the time and place of such meeting.

§ 47. Seniority among the trustees shall be determined according to the order in which they are named in the charter of the college; and after all the first trustees shall become extinct, according to the priority of their election.

§ 48. The trustees shall not exceed twenty-four, nor be less than ten, in number; and a majority of the whole number, shall be a quorum for the transaction of business.

§ 49. The trustees of every such college, besides the general powers and privileges of a corporation, shall have power,

1. To elect by ballot their chairman annually:

2. Upon the death, removal out of this state, or other vacancy in the office of any trustee, to elect another in his place by a majority of the votes of the trustees present:

3. To declare vacant the seat of any trustee, who shall absent himself from five successive meetings of the board:

4. To take and hold, by gift, grant or devise, any real or personal property, the yearly income or revenue of which shall not exceed the value of twenty-five thousand dollars:

5. To sell, mortgage, let and otherwise use and dispose of such property in such manner, as they shall deem most conducive to the interest of the college:

6. To direct and prescribe the course of study and discipline, to be observed in the college:

7. To appoint a president of the college, who shall hold his office during good behavior:

8. To appoint such professors, trustees and other officers, as they shall deem necessary; who, unless employed under a special contract, shall hold their offices during the pleasure of the trustees:

9. To remove or suspend from office the president and every professor, tutor, or other officer employed under a special contract, upon a complaint in writing by any member of the board of trustees, stating the misbehavior in office, incapacity or immoral conduct, of the person sought to be removed, and upon examination and due proof of the truth of such complaint; and to appoint any other person in place of the president or other officer, thus removed or suspended:

least once at any of the meetings of the regents to be held during any session of the legislature, when by law they are required to meet, without some just cause satisfactory to the board of regents, such non-attendance shall be deemed a resignation of their seats; and it shall be the duty of the regents to report to the legislature, from time to time, the names of the members whose seats shall thus become vacant, to the end that the same may be supplied.

10. To grant such literary honors as are usually granted by any university, college, or seminary of learning in the United States; and in testimony thereof, to give suitable diplomas, under their seal, and the signature of such officers of the college as they shall deem expedient:

11. To ascertain and fix the salaries of the president, professors and other officers of the college:

12. To make all ordinances and by-laws necessary and proper to carry into effect the preceding powers.

§ 50. Every diploma granted by such trustees shall entitle the possessor to all the immunities which by usage or statute are allowed to possessors of similar diplomas granted by any university, college, or seminary of learning in the United States.

ARTICLE THIRD.

Of the foundation of academies.

SEC. 51. Founders of an academy may apply to regents for incorporation.
52. How approbation of regents declared.
53. When funds vest and how.

§ 51. The founders and benefactors of an academy, or as many of them as shall have contributed more than one-half in value of the property collected for the use thereof, may make to the regents an application in writing under their hands, requesting that such academy may be incorporated, nominating the first trustees, and specifying the name by which the corporation is to be called.

§ 52. In case the regents shall approve thereof, they shall, by an instrument under their common seal, declare their approbation of the incorporation of the trustees of such academy, by the name specified in such application; and the request, and instrument of approbation, shall be recorded in the office of the secretary of state.

§ 53. Immediately after recording the same, the property and funds of such academy shall be vested in the trustees so nominated, for the use and benefit of the academy.

ARTICLE FOURTH.

Of the powers and duties of trustees of academies.

SEC. 54. Trustees to be a corporation; name; number; what number a quorum.
55. Powers of trustees enumerated.
56. How meetings summoned, and by whom.
57. Time and place, how appointed.
58. How notice to be given; who to preside.
59. How seniority determined.
60. In what case the office of a trustee may be vacated.
61. Absence for a year to be deemed a resignation.
62 & 63. How their number may be reduced.

§ 54. The trustees of every such academy shall be a corporation, by the name expressed in the instrument of approbation: they shall not be more than twenty-four, nor less than twelve, in number; and seven trustees of any academy shall be a quorum for the transaction of business. [*Amended by* § 3 *of chap.* 34 *of* 1835.]*

§ 55. Such trustees, besides the general powers and privileges of a corporation, shall have authority,

1. To adjourn from time to time, as they may deem expedient:

2. To elect by ballot their president, who shall hold his office for one year, and until another be chosen in his place:

3. Upon the death, resignation, refusal to act, removal out of this State, or other vacancy in the office of any trustee, to elect another in his place, by a majority of the votes of the trustees present:

4. To take and hold by gift, grant or devise, any real or personal property, the clear yearly income or revenue of which shall not exceed the value of four thousand dollars:

5. To sell, mortgage, let, or otherwise use and dispose of such property, for the benefit of the academy:

6. To direct and prescribe the course of discipline and study in the academy:

7. To appoint a treasurer, clerk, principal, masters, tutors, and other necessary officers of the academy; who, unless employed under a special contract, shall hold their offices during the pleasure of the trustees:

8. To ascertain and fix the salaries of all the officers of the academy:

9. To remove or suspend from office any officer employed under a special contract, upon a complaint in writing by a trustee, of the misbehavior in office, incapacity or immoral conduct of such officer, and upon examination and due proof of the truth of such complaint, and to appoint another person in the place of such officer so removed or suspended:

10. To make all ordinances and by-laws necessary and proper to carry into effect the preceding powers.

§ 56. The trustees shall meet upon their own adjournment, and as often as they shall be summoned by their president, or the senior trustee actually exercising his office and residing within three miles of such academy, upon the request in writing of any other three trustees.

§ 57. Every meeting so requested shall be held at such time and place as the president or senior trustee shall appoint, not less than five nor more than twelve days from the time of the request.

§ 58. Previous notice in writing of every such meeting shall be fixed on the door of the academy, within two days after its appointment; and at every meeting, adjourned or special, the president or senior trustee present shall preside.

§ 59. The seniority of the trustees shall always be determined

* The words of section 3 of chapter 34 of 1835 are as follows: "Seven trustees of any academy shall be a quorum for the transaction of business; and so much of the forty-first section of the first title of chapter fifteen of the first part of the Revised Statutes as requires a majority of the whole number of trustees for a quorum for the transaction of business, is hereby repealed."

according to the order of their nomination in the written application to the regents; and after all the first trustees shall become extinct, according to the priority of their election.

§ 60. If a trustee shall refuse or neglect to attend any two successive legal meetings of the trustees, after having been personally notified to attend, and if no satisfactory cause of his non-attendance be shown, the trustees may declare his office vacant.

§ 61. If any trustee of an academy shall, for one year, refuse or neglect to attend the legal meetings of the board of trustees of which he is a member, such non-attendance shall be deemed a resignation of the office of such trustee. [*Sec.* 2 *of chap.* 123 *of* 1835.]

§ 62. Where the number of trustees of any academy shall exceed twelve, the trustees thereof, at their annual meeting, may reduce the number of the original board of trustees to any number not less than twelve, by abolishing the offices of those who may omit to attend such meeting, and shall have omitted to attend two other legal meetings after notice.

§ 63. Where the number of trustees of any academy shall exceed twelve, and a vacancy shall happen in the office of any such trustees, and the vacancy shall not be filled by the election of another trustee within six months after the happening of such vacancy, the office of the trustee so becoming vacant shall be abolished. [*Sec.* 3 *of chap.* 123 *of* 1835.]

ARTICLE FIFTH.

General provisions applicable to colleges and academies.

Sec. 64. No religious qualification to be required in professors, tutors, &c.
65. No professor or tutor to be a trustee.
66. No president or principal has a vote relative to his own emoluments.
67. No officer to be a regent.
68. No trustee to be a regent, or regent a trustee.
69. Returns to be made by institutions.
70. Nothing in this Chapter to affect any charter heretofore granted.
71. Article 4th applied to certain academies.

§ 64. No religious qualification or test shall be required from any trustee, president, principal, or other officer of any incorporated college or academy, or as a condition for admission to any privilege in the same.

§ 65. No professor or tutor of any incorporated college or academy, shall be a trustee of such college or academy.

§ 66. No president of any such college, or principal of any such academy, who shall be a trustee, shall have a vote in any case relating to his own salary or emoluments.

§ 67. No president, principal, or other officer of any such college or academy, shall be a regent of the university.

§ 68. No trustee of a college or academy shall act as a regent of the university, and no regent of the university shall act as trustee of any college or academy; and if any such trustee shall be appointed a regent, or a regent shall be appointed a trustee, he shall elect in which office he will serve, and give notice of such election to the authority by which he shall be appointed, within sixty days from the time of his appointment, otherwise such appointment shall be void.

§ 69. Every college and academy that shall become subject to the visitation of the regents shall make such returns and reports to the regents, in relation to the state and disposition of its property and funds, the number and ages of its pupils, and its system of instruction and discipline, as the regents shall from time to time require.

§ 70. Nothing contained in this chapter shall be construed to alter, or in any manner affect any charter heretofore granted by the legislature, or by the regents of the university, to any college or academy.

§ 71. Nothing in the seventieth section of the first title of chapter fifteen, part first of the Revised Statutes, shall be construed to prevent article fourth of said title from extending and applying to the trustees of all academies incorporated by the regents of the university prior to the first day of January, one thousand eight hundred and thirty. [*Sec.* 1 *of chap.* 123 *of* 1835.]

ARTICLE SIXTH.

Of the foundation and government of Lancasterian and select schools.

§ 72. The founders and benefactors of any school established or to be established for the instruction of youth, on the system of Lancaster or Bell, or any other system of instruction approved by the board of regents, or as many of such founders as shall have contributed more than one-half of the property collected or appropriated for the use of such school, may make to the regents of the university an application in writing under their hands, requesting that such school may be incorporated, nominating the first trustees, and specifying the name by which the corporation is to be called.

§ 73. In case the regents shall conceive a compliance with such request will be conducive to the diffusion of useful knowledge, they shall, by an instrument under their common seal, declare their approbation of the incorporation of the trustees of the school, by the name specified in such application.

§ 74. The request in writing, and instrument of approbation, shall be recorded in the office of the clerk of the county in which such school shall be established.

§ 75. Immediately after recording the same, the property and funds of such school shall be vested in the trustees so nominated, for the use and benefit of the school.

§ 76. The trustees of such school shall be a corporation, by the name expressed in the instrument of approbation.

§ 77. The trustees of every such school (besides the general powers and privileges of a corporation) shall have authority,

1. To elect by ballot their president, treasurer and clerk annually:

2. Upon the death, resignation, refusal to act, removal out of the State, or other vacancy in the office of any trustee, to elect another in his place:

3. To appoint a master, assistants, and other necessary officers of the school:

4. To remove or suspend any of them at pleasure, and to fix their respective salaries or compensation:

5. To appoint the times and places of their own regular meetings, and to adjourn from time to time:

6. To take and hold any real or personal property, the clear yearly income or revenue of which shall not exceed the value of four thousand dollars:

7. To sell, mortgage, let, and otherwise use and dispose of such property for the benefit of the school:

8. To make all ordinances and by-laws necessary and proper to carry into effect the preceding powers.

§ 78. If any trustee shall refuse or neglect to attend the stated meetings of the trustees for four meetings successively, the office of such trustee may be declared vacant by the trustees.

§ 79. The trustees of one or more common school districts in any city, town or village of this State, within which any incorporated Lancasterian or other select school is or shall be established, with the consent of a majority of the taxable inhabitants of such district or districts, expressed at a meeting called for that purpose, may agree with the trustees of such incorporated school to make the same a district school.

§ 80. Such incorporated school shall, during the continuance of such agreement, become a district school, and be entitled to all the benefits and privileges, and subject to all the regulations of other district schools.

§ 81. Every school incorporated under the provisions of this article shall be subject to the control and visitation of the regents; and shall make such returns and reports in relation to the state and disposition of its property and funds, the number and ages of its pupils, and its system of instruction and discipline, as the regents shall from time to time require.

ACTS OR PARTS OF ACTS NOT REVISED, AND STILL IN FORCE.

(See Revised Statutes, 3rd Ed. Vol. 3. p. 222.)

An act relative to the University. Passed April 5, 1813. Chap. 59.

§ 1. *Be it enacted by the People of the State of New-York, represented in Senate and Assembly,* That an university be, and is hereby instituted within this State, to be called and known by the name or style of *The Regents of the University of the State of New-York*, that the said regents shall always be twenty-one in number, of which the governor and lieutenant-governor of the State, for the time being, shall always, in virtue of their offices, be two; that the governor, lieutenant-governor, and Matthew Clarkson, Andrew King, Lucus Elmendorf, James Kent, James Cochran, Abraham Van Vechten, Simeon De Witt, Henry Rutgers, De Witt Clinton, Alexander Sheldon, Charles Selden, Nathan Smith, John Taylor, Elisha Jenkins, Ambrose Spencer, Joseph C. Yates, Solomon Southwick, Smith Thompson and John Woodworth, shall be, and hereby are appointed the present regents; and that they and all the future regents shall continue in place during the pleasure of the legislature; that all vacancies in the regency which may happen by death or removal, or resignation, shall from time to time, be supplied by the legislature in the manner in which senators in the congress of the United States are appointed; that the said regents shall convene at such time and place as the governor shall appoint, and by plurality of voices, by ballot, choose a chancellor and vice-chancellor, to continue in office during the pleasure of the said regents; that the said chancellor, or in his absence from the said meeting, the vice-chancellor, or in case both be absent, then the senior regent present (and whose seniority shall be decided by the order in which the regents are named or appointed) shall preside, and in case of division, have a casting vote at all meetings of the said regents: that all meetings of the said regents, after the said first meeting to be called by the governor as aforesaid, shall be held at such time and place as the chancellor, or in case of his death, absence from the State, or resignation, the vice-chancellor, or in case of the death, absence from the State, or resignation of both of them, then at such time and place as the senior regent present in the State shall appoint; and it shall be the duty of the chancellor, vice-chancellor, or senior regent, as the case in virtue of the above contingencies may be, to order and call a meeting of the said regents whenever and as often as three regents shall, in writing, apply for and request the same, such order or call to be published in one or more of the public newspapers in the city of Albany, at least ten days prior to such meeting: *And further*, that any eight of the said regents meeting, at the time and place so ordered, shall be a quorum, and be enabled to transact and do the business, which by this act they shall be authorised or directed to do and transact; that the said university shall be and hereby is incorporated, and shall be known by the name of The Regents of the University of the State of New-York, and by that name shall have perpetual succession and power to sue and be sued, to hold property real and personal, to the amount of the annual income of forty thousand bushels of wheat, to buy and to sell, and otherwise lawfully dispose of lands and chattels, to make and use a common seal, and to alter the same at pleasure.

§ 2. *And be it further enacted*, That the said corporation shall appoint by ballot, a treasurer and a secretary, to continue in office during the pleasure of the corporation; that the treasurer shall keep fair and true accounts of all monies by him received and paid out, and that the secretary shall keep a fair journal of the meetings and proceedings of the corporation, in which the yeas and nays on all questions shall be entered, if required by any one of the regents present; and to all the books and papers of the corporation every regent shall always have access, and be permitted to take copies of them.

§ 3. *And be it further enacted*, That it shall and may be lawful to and for the said regents, and they are hereby authorised and required to visit and inspect all the colleges, academies, and schools which are or may be established in this State, examine into the state and system of education and discipline therein, and make a yearly report thereof to the legislature, and also to visit every college in this State once a year, by themselves or by their committees, and yearly to report the state of the same to the legislature, and to make such by-laws and ordinances, not inconsistent with the constitution and laws of this State, as they may judge most expedient for the accomplishment of the trust hereby reposed in them; and in case the trustees of the said colleges, or any of them, shall leave the office of president of the college, or the trustees of any academy, shall leave the office or place of principal of the academy vacant, for the space of one year, it shall, in all such cases, be lawful for the regents, unless a reasonable cause shall be assigned for such delay to their satisfaction, to fill up such vacancies; and the person by them appointed shall continue in office during the pleasure of the regents, and shall respectively be received by the college or academy to which they may be appointed, and shall have all the powers and the same salary, emoluments and privileges, as his next immediate predecessor in office enjoyed, if any predecessor he had, if not, then such salary as the regents shall direct, to be paid by the trustees, who shall out of the funds or estate of their college or academy, be compellable by the said president or principal to pay the same.

§ 4. *And be it further enacted*, That it shall and may be lawful to and for the said regents, from time to time, to apply such part of their estate and funds in such manner as they may think most conducive to the promotion of literature and the advancement of useful knowledge within this State: provided always that where grants shall be made to them for certain uses and purposes therein expressed and declared, the same shall not be applied, either in the whole or in part, to any other uses.

§ 5. *And be it further enacted*, That the regents shall annually meet on the second Thursday next after the senate and assembly at the annual session of the legislature, shall have formed a quorum respectively, and at the assembly chamber, immediately after the assembly shall have adjourned; that the said regents, at such meetings and all others, may adjourn from time to time, not exceeding ten days at any one time.

§ 6. *And be it further enacted*, That any citizen or citizens, or bodies corporate within this State, being disposed to found a college at any place within the same, he or they shall, in writing, make known to the regents, the place where, the plan on which, and the funds with which, it is intended to found and provide for the same, and who are proposed for the first trustees; and in case the regents shall approve thereof, then they shall declare their approbation by an instrument under their common seal, and allow a convenient time for completing the same; and if at the expiration of the said time, it shall appear to the satisfaction of the regents, that the said plan and propositions are fully executed, then they shall, by act under their common seal, declare that the said college, to be named as the founders shall signify, and with such trustees not exceeding twenty-four, nor less than ten, as they shall name, shall forthwith become incorporated, and shall have perpetual succession, and enjoy all the corporate rights and privileges enjoyed by Columbia college, in and by the act entitled "An act to institute an university within this State, and for other purposes therein mentioned," passed April 13, 1787.

§ 7. *And be it further enacted*, That the said regents shall have the right of conferring by diplomas, under their common seal, on any person or persons whom they may think worthy thereof, all such degrees, above or beyond those of bachelor or master of arts, as are known to, and usually granted by, any university or college in Europe, and the degree of doctor of medicine granted by the said regents, shall authorise the person on whom it is conferred to practice physic and surgery in this State, any thing in any law to the contrary notwithstanding.

§ 8. *And be it further enacted*, That the charter granted to the college of physicians and surgeons in the city of New-York, by the regents of the university, bearing date the fourth day of June, one thousand eight hundred and twelve, be and the same is hereby ratified and confirmed, any grant or charter heretofore made by the said regents to the said college to the contrary notwithstanding: *Provided always*, That the amount of the property which the said college shall or may be authorised to hold, shall never exceed in value one hundred and fifty thousand dollars, current money of New-York; and that the said regents reserve to themselves the right of conferring degrees, and appointing the professors or teachers of the several branches of the medical science in the said college, and of filling all such vacancies as shall or may arise among the trustees or members thereof: *And provided also*, That any of the trustees of the said college shall, in the discretion of the regents of the university, be appointed professors and teachers in the said college, any law to the contrary notwithstanding.

§ 9. *And be it further enacted*, That it shall be lawful for the said regents, at any time or times hereafter, to alter and amend the said charter, provided such alterations or amendments be not repugnant to the constitution or laws of this State, or inconsistent with vested interests.

§ 10. *And be it further enacted*, That upon the application of the founders and benefactors of any academy, now or hereafter to be erected or established within any of the cities or counties of this State, or as many of them as shall have contributed more than one half in value of the real and personal property and estate, collected and appropriated for the use and benefit thereof, by an instrument in writing under their hands and seals to the regents of the university, expressing their request that such academy should be incorporated, and be subject to the visitation of the regents, nominating in such instrument the trustees, not more than twenty-four nor less than twelve, for such academy, and specifying the name by which the said trustees shall be called and distinguished; and whenever any such request shall be made to the said regents, they shall, in every such case, (if they conceive such academy calculated for the promotion of literature) by an instrument under their common seal, signify their approbation of the incorporation of the trustees of such academy, named by the founders thereof by the name mentioned in and by their said request in writing, which said request in writing and instrument of approbation by the said regents, shall be recorded in the secretary's office of the State

§ 11. *And be it further enacted*, That the trustees so constituted, shall be the first trustees for the academy for which they shall be appointed, and immediately after recording the said request in writing and instrument of approbation, shall be legally invested with all the real and personal estate appertaining to such academy, or in any wise given or granted for the use thereof; and the said trustees, from the time of their appointment as aforesaid, and their successors forever thereafter, shall be a body corporate and politic, in deed, fact and name, known and distinguished by the name and style to be expressed in the said instrument, and by that name shall have perpetual succession, and be capable in the law to sue and be sued, and defend and be defended, in all courts and in all causes, plaints, controversies, matters and things whatsoever, and by the same name and style, they and their successors shall lawfully hold, use and enjoy, the lands, tenements and hereditaments in any wise appertaining to the academy for which they shall be constituted trustees, and shall and may lawfully have, take, acquire, purchase and enjoy, lands, tenements and hereditaments, and use and improve such goods and chattels, in such manner as they shall judge to be the most beneficial for such academy: provided that the annual revenue or income arising from the real and personal estate of any such academy, shall not exceed the value of four thousand bushels of wheat, any law, usage, or custom, to the contrary notwithstanding.

§ 12. *And be it further enacted*, That it shall and may be lawful to, and for such trustees and their successors forever, to have and use a common seal, and the same to alter, break and make anew at their pleasure; and as often as any three or more of the said trustees shall think fit, and signify their request, the senior trustee actually exercising his office, and residing within three miles of such academy, shall call a meeting of the said trustees, at such convenient time and place as he shall appoint, not less than eight nor more than twelve days from the time of such request, of which previous notice in writing shall be affixed on the door of the academy and of the church nearest thereto, within two days after such appointment; and at every such meeting the senior trustee shall preside, such seniority in all cases to be determined according to the order of their nomination in the said instrument, or according to the priority of election after all the first trustees shall become extinct; and the major part of such trustees shall always be a sufficient quorum to proceed on business, and shall have full power and authority to adjourn from time to time, as the duties of their trust may require; and it shall and may be lawful to and for such quorum of the said trustees, when assembled and met in manner aforesaid, or the major part of them, from time to time to appoint a treasurer and clerk, principal, masters, tutors, teachers and other necessary officers, to ascertain their respective salaries, and to remove and displace any of them at their pleasure, and to make by-laws for the admission, education, government and discipline of the scholars and students, and the establishment of the price or terms of tuition, for securing, revising and paying out and disposing of the revenues, and in general for conducting and managing the estate, business and affairs of the said academy, and every matter and thing relating thereto, in such manner as they shall judge to be most conducive to its interests and prosperity, and the end of their trust.

§ 13. *And be it further enacted*, That whenever a vacancy shall happen in any corporation of trustees by the death, resignation or refusal to act, of any trustee, it shall and may be lawful to and for the trustees of such academy, and they are hereby authorised and required at any legal meeting of the trustees to elect and choose a fit person to fill up and supply such vacancy.

§ 14. *And be it further enacted*, That the regents of the university, the chancellor, vice-chancellor or a committee of the regents, shall be visitors of all academies as often as they see proper to inquire into the state and progress of literature therein.

§ 15. *And be it further enacted*, That when any scholar who shall be educated at any of the said academies, on due examination, by the president and professors of any college subject to the visitation of the said regents, shall be found competent, in the judgment of the said president and professors, to enter into the sophomore, junior or senior classes of such colleges, respectively, such scholar shall be entitled to an admission into such of the said classes, for which he shall be so adjudged competent, and shall be admitted accordingly at any one of the quarterly examinations of such respective classes.

§ 16. *Provided always, and be it further enacted*, That to entitle the scholars of any such academy to the privileges aforesaid, the trustees thereof shall lay before the regents of the said university, from time to time, the plan or system proposed to be adopted for the education of the students in each of the said academies respectively, in order that the same may be revised and examined by the said regents, and by them be altered or amended, or approved and confirmed, as they shall judge proper.

§ 17. *And be it further enacted*, That whenever it shall appear to the said regents that the state of literature in any academy is so far advanced, and the funds will admit thereof, that it may be expedient that a president be appointed for such academy, the said regents shall in such case signify their approbation thereof, under their common seal; which being entered of record as aforesaid, shall authorise the trustees of such academy to elect a president, who shall have, hold and enjoy all the powers that the president of any college recognized by this act, shall or may lawfully have, hold and enjoy; and such academy thereafter, instead of being called an academy, shall be called and known by the same name it was called while it was an academy, except that the word college shall be used in all cases, instead of the word academy, and be subject to the like rules, regulations, control and visitation of the regents, as other colleges mentioned in this act.

§ 18. *And be it further enacted*, That no president or professor shall be ineligible for or by reason of any religious tenet or tenets that he may or shall profess, or be compelled by any law or otherwise to take any test oath whatsoever; and no professor or tutor of any college or academy recognized by this act, shall be a trustee of any such college or academy; nor shall any president of any college or principal of any academy who shall be a trustee, have a vote in any case relating to his own salary or emoluments; nor shall any trustee, president, principal, tutor, fellow or other officer of any college or academy be a regent of the university.

§ 19. *And be it further enacted*, That whenever any person now or hereafter appointed a trustee of any college or academy shall be appointed or elected a regent of the university, and whenever any person being a regent of the university shall be appointed or elected a trustee of any college or academy, such person so appointed or elected shall, on due notice thereof, decide and elect in which of the said places he will serve, and by writing under his hand, shall make known such election, whether of refusal or acceptance, to those by whom he was elected, to the end that such appointment may take effect in case he accept it, or that they proceed to a new appointment in case he refuse it.

§ 20. *And be it further enacted*, That it shall and may be lawful for the trustees of any incorporated academy within this State, when legally convened, to choose by a majority of votes, one of their body as president, for one year, or until another shall be chosen in his room, which president, so chosen, may do and perform all the duties required to be done by the senior trustee of such academy, in pursuance of this act.

In the Revised Statutes as above referred to, only the 6th, 8th, 9th, 15th, 16th and 17th sections of the above Law are published, as not revised. The whole of the act is however here given for convenience of reference and comparison.

An act relating to the different colleges within this State. Passed April 9, 1813. Chap. 82.

(See Revised Statutes, 3d Ed., Vol. 3, p. 224.)

§ 1. *Be it enacted by the People of the State of New-York, represented in Senate and Assembly*, That the present trustees of Columbia college, and their successors, shall be and remain forever hereafter, a body politic and corporate, in fact and in name, by the name of "The trustees of Columbia college in the city of New-York," and by that name shall and may have continual succession forever hereafter, and shall be able in law to sue and be sued, implead and be impleaded, answer and be answered unto, defend and be defended in all courts and places whatsoever, and may have a common seal, and may change and alter the same at their pleasure; and also shall be able in law to take by purchase, gift, grant, devise or in any other manner, and to hold any real or personal estate whatsoever: provided always the clear yearly value of the real estate to be so acquired, shall not exceed the sum of twenty thousand dollars, and also that they and their successors shall have power to give, grant, bargain, sell, demise or otherwise dispose of, all or any part of the said real and personal estate as to them shall seem best for the interest of the said college.

§ 2. *And be it further enacted*, That the said trustees and their successors shall forever hereafter have full power and authority to direct and prescribe the course of study, and the discipline to be observed in the said college; and also to select and appoint by ballot or otherwise a president of the said college, who shall hold his office during good behavior, and such professor or professors, tutor or tutors, to assist the president in the government and education of the students belonging to the said college, and such other officer or officers as to the said trustees shall seem meet, all of whom shall hold their offices during the pleasure of the trustees: provided always that no such professor, tutor or other assistant officer shall be a trustee, but this proviso shall not extend to the provost of the said college, for the time being, who is hereby declared eligible as a trustee of said college.

§ 3. *And be it further enacted,* That if complaint shall be made, in writing, to the said trustees or their successors, by any member of the said corporation, of any misbehavior in office by the president, it shall be lawful for the said trustees or their successors from time to time, upon examination and such due proof of misbehavior, to suspend or discharge such president, and to appoint another in his place.

§ 4. *And be it further enacted,* That eleven of the said trustees lawfully convened as is hereinafter directed, shall be a quorum for the despatch of all business, except for the disposal of real estate, or for the choice or removal of a president, for either of which purposes there shall be a meeting of at least thirteen trustees.

§ 5 *And be it further enacted,* That the said trustees shall have full power and authority to elect, by ballot, their own chairman, once in every year, or at such other periods as they shall prefer.

§ 6. *And be it further enacted,* That the said trustees shall also have power, by a majority of the votes of the members present, to elect and appoint, upon the death, removal out of the State, or other vacancy of the place or places of any trustee or trustees, other or others in his or their places or stead, as often as such vacancy shall happen; and also to make and declare vacant the seat of any trustee who shall absent himself from five successive meetings of the board, and also to meet upon their own adjournment, and so often as they shall be summoned by their chairman, or in his absence, by the senior trustee, whose seniority shall be accounted according to the order in which the said trustees are named in this act, and shall be elected hereafter: provided always that the said chairman or senior trustee shall not summon a meeting of the corporation, unless required thereto, in writing, by three of the members: *And provided also,* That he cause notice of the time and place of said meeting to be given, in one or more of the public newspapers printed in the city of New-York, at least three days before such meeting; and that every member of the corporation, resident in the city, shall be previously advertised in writing, of the time and place of every such meeting.

§ 7. *And be it further enacted,* That the said trustees and their successors shall have power and authority to grant all such literary honors and degrees, as are usually granted by any university, college or seminary of learning, in this State or the United States; and in testimony of such grant, to give suitable diplomas, under their seal and the signatures of the president and such professors or tutors of the college as they shall judge expedient; which diplomas shall entitle the possessors respectively to all the immunities and privileges which, either by usage or statute, are allowed to possessors of similar diplomas, from any university, college or seminary of learning.

§ 8. *And be it further enacted*, That the said trustees and their successors shall have full power and authority to make all ordinances and by-laws which to them shall seem expedient, for carrying into effect the designs of their institution: provided always that such ordinances or by-laws shall not make the religious tenets of any person a condition of admission to any privilege or office in the said college, nor be inconsistent with the constitution and laws of this State, nor with the constitution and laws of the United States.

§ 9. *And be it further enacted*, That all the real and personal estate whatsoever and wheresoever, which was formerly vested in the governors of the college of the province of New-York, in the city of New-York, in America, or in the trustees of Columbia college, in the city of New-York, be and the same is hereby confirmed to and vested in the said trustees of Columbia college, in the city of New-York, and their successors forever, for the sole use and benefit of the said college; and that it shall and may be lawful to and for the said trustees and their successors, to grant, bargain, sell, demise, improve and dispose of the same, as to them shall seem meet: provided always that the lands given and granted to the governors of the college of the province of New-York, in the city of New-York, in America, by the corporation heretofore styled "The rector and inhabitants of the city of New-York, in communion of the church of England, as by law established," on part whereof said college is erected, shall not be granted for any greater term of time than sixty-three years.

§ 10. *And be it further enacted*, That the agreement made between the trustees of Union college, in the city of Schenectady, and the mayor, aldermen and commonalty of the said city, relative to the purchase or exchange of certain real estate lying within the bounds of the said city, be and the same is hereby confirmed and declared valid in law, to every intent and purpose therein expressed and declared, any law to the contrary notwithstanding.

§ 11. *And be it further enacted*, That the sum of thirty-five thousand dollars, heretofore paid to the trustees of the said college out of the avails of certain lotteries, shall be and remain at interest, payable annually, on approved landed security, or shall be invested in public stock, in such manner as the trustees of said college, from time to time, by and with the consent, in writing, of the person administering the government of this State, or the chancellor thereof, shall direct and prescribe; and the annual income of such sum shall forever hereafter be solely and exclusively applied for the support of such professorships as are or may be instituted in the said college; and that it shall not be lawful for the said trustees or their successors, at any time hereafter, to lessen the said principal sum of thirty-five thousand dollars, or to appropriate the same, or any part thereof, to or for any use or purpose whatsoever; and the said trustees shall annually exhibit to the legislature a just, true and circumstantial account of their proceedings in relation to the disposition and application of the interest that shall accrue from the said principal sum of thirty-five thousand dollars, and how the said principal sum is invested, or to whom, and on what security, placed at interest.

§ 12. *And be it further enacted*, That thirty-five thousand dollars, also paid, or to be paid, to the trustees, out of the avails of certain lotteries, shall be applied towards the erection of such additional edifices for the accommodation of the students in the said college, as they shall deem proper; and ten thousand dollars, also paid, or to be paid, the said trustees, out of the avails of certain lotteries, shall be invested or put out at interest, in the manner declared in the preceding section, one-half of the income whereof to be laid out by the said trustees in establishing and maintaining forever a classical library, from which library all the students in the seminary shall be furnished with the books which they are required to study, subject to such regulations as the board of trustees shall prescribe, paying for the use of the same one dollar and fifty cents per quarter: *And further*, All indigent students who shall make it appear to the faculty of the college that they are embarrassed for the want of pecuniary resources, shall, during good behavior, be furnished, free of expense, with the books necessary for pursuing their education: *And further*, The remaining half of the income of the said ten thousand dollars shall forever be appropriated towards defraying the expenses of such indigent scholars as may be, from time to time, pursuing their education in said seminary.

§ 13. *And be it further enacted*, That the number of trustees of said college shall not exceed twenty-one in number, and of that number the chancellor, the justices of the supreme court, the secretary of State, the comptroller, the treasurer, the attorney-general and the surveyor-general for the time being, shall respectively be *ex officio* trustees of said college: *And further*, The regents of the university are authorised to fill all vacancies of the said trustees, from time to time to take place, but nothing herein contained shall prevent the present trustees from holding and enjoying their said trust.

§ 14. *And be it further enacted*, That the grants of funds and land heretofore made to the said college by the people of this State, be and hereby are confirmed; but all former responsibilities and engagements of the said college to the people of this State, by reason of any monies borrowed or advanced, shall be and remain in like manner as if this act had not been passed.

§ 15. *And be it further enacted*, That it shall not be lawful for any person to entice the students of the Union college, or of the grammar school belonging to the same, into the vice of gaming, by keeping within the first and second wards of the city of Schenectady, any billiard-table or other instrument or device for the purpose of gaming, and that if any person shall keep any billiard-table or other instrument or device for gaming within the aforesaid first and second wards of the city of Schenectady, or shall entice or permit any student of Union college, or of the grammar-school belonging to the same, to game or play at the said billiard-table or other instrument or device aforesaid, or shall entice or permit them, or any of them, to enter the place where the same is kept, every person so offending shall forfeit the sum of twenty-five dollars for every such offence, to be recovered in an action of debt in any court having cognizance thereof, the one moiety to the use of the people of this State, and the other to the benefit of such person as shall prosecute therefore.

§ 16. *And be it further enacted*, That it shall be the duty of the sheriff of the county, together with the constables of the said city of Schenectady, to attend the annual commencement and the public exhibitions of the said Union college, to preserve peace and good order, and prevent any unlawful assemblage and tumult about the same.

SESSION LAWS RELATIVE TO THE UNIVERSITY, COLLEGES, ACADEMIES, &c.

SESSION LAWS OF 1840.

CHAPTER 318. *An act authorising certain trusts.*

Passed May 14, 1840.

The People of the State of New-York, represented in Senate and Assembly, do enact as follows:

Sec. 1. Real and personal property may be granted and conveyed to any incorporated college, or other literary incorporated institution in this State, to be held in trust for either of the following purposes:

1. To establish and maintain an observatory;
2. To found and maintain professorships and scholarships;
3. To provide and keep in repair a place for the burial of the dead;
4. For any other specific purposes comprehended in the general objects authorised by their respective charters.

The said trusts may be created, subject to such conditions and visitations as may be prescribed by the grantor or donor, and agreed to by said trustees; and all property which shall hereafter be granted to any incorporated college or other literary incorporated institution in trust for either of the aforesaid purposes, may be held by such college or institution upon such trusts and subject to such conditions and visitations as may be prescribed and agreed to as aforesaid.

§ 2. Real and personal property may be granted and conveyed to the corporation of any city or village of this State, to be held in trust for any purpose of education, or the diffusion of knowledge, or for the relief of distress, or for parks, gardens or other ornamental grounds, or grounds for the purposes of military parades and exercise, or health and recreation, within or near such incorporated city or village, upon such conditions as may be prescribed by the grantor or donor, and agreed to by such corporation; and all real estate so granted or conveyed to such corporation may be held by the same, subject to such conditions as may be prescribed and agreed to as aforesaid.

§ 3. Real and personal estate may be granted to commissioners of common schools of any town and to trustees of any school district, in trust for the benefit of the common schools of such town, or for the benefit of the schools of such district.

§ 4. The trusts authorised by this act may continue for such time as may be necessary to accomplish the purposes for which they may be created.

SESSION LAWS OF 1841.

CHAPTER 261. *An act in addition to "An act authorising certain trusts," passed May* 14, 1840.

Passed May 26, 1841.

The People of the State of New-York, represented in Senate and Assembly, do enact as follows:

§ 1. Devises and bequests of real and personal property in trust for any of the purposes for which such trusts are authorised under the "Act authorising certain trusts," passed May 14, 1840, and to such trustees as are therein authorised, shall be valid in like manner as if such property had been granted and conveyed according to the provisions of the aforesaid act.

SESSION LAWS OF 1846.

CHAPTER 74. *An act to amend the act passed May,* 1841, *authorising colleges and other incorporated literary institutions to hold real and personal estate in trust, so as to allow the same to accumulate for certain specific purposes.*

Passed April 21, 1846.

The People of the State of New-York, represented in Senate and Assembly, do enact as follows:

§ 1. The income arising from any real or personal property granted or conveyed, devised or bequeathed in trust to any incorporated college or other incorporated literary institution, for any of the purposes specified in the "act authorising certain trusts," passed May 14, 1840, or for the purpose of providing for the support of any teacher in a grammar school or institute, may be permitted to accumulate till the same shall amount to a sum sufficient, in the opinion of the regents of the University, to carry into effect either of the purposes aforesaid, designated in said trust.

[These three last laws are also to be found in the Revised Statutes, 3d edition, Vol. 2, pages 23 and 24.]

NATURAL HISTORY OF NEW-YORK.

CHAPTER 132. *An act concerning the Natural History of the State of New-York.*

Passed May 5, 1846.

The People of the State of New-York, represented in Senate and Assembly, do enact as follows:

§ 1. The Secretary of State is hereby authorised and directed to sell to such of the academies, public libraries and literary associations in this State which are now incorporated, as shall have made or which shall make application therefor, a copy of the Natural History of this State, at the price of one dollar per volume, and a copy of the Geological map of the State, at the price of one dollar per copy, out of the remaining three hundred copies of the said volumes and maps reserved for that purpose by the second section of the act entitled "An act in relation to the Natural History of New-York," passed May 3, 1844, but no sale of the said volumes and map shall be made by the said Secretary of State, after the expiration of one year after the passage of this act, nor a second copy to an institution which has received a copy of the said work under the provisions of chap. 254, of the laws of 1844.

CHAPTER 190. *Session Laws of* 1847. Passed May 5, 1847.

§ 1. The provisions contained in the last recited law, are hereby continued and shall be in force for the term of one year from the passage of this act, and the Secretary of State is directed to sell to such of the institutions named in the first section of the above mentioned act, which now are or hereafter may be incorporated during the continuance of this act, copies of the Natural History of this State, upon the conditions and subject to the restrictions therein contained.

CHAPTER. 266. *Session Laws of* 1849. Passed April 7, 1849.

The provisions as above, are continued and shall be in force for the term of two years from the passage of this act.

CHAPTER 366. *Session Laws of* 1852. Passed April 16, 1852.

The provisions as above are continued and shall be in force for the term of two years from the passage of this act, and the Secretary is authorised and directed to sell to the institutions above named, *which now are incorporated*, during the continuance of this act, copies of the Natural History, &c.

SESSION LAWS.

CHAPTER 544. *An act to incorporate Academies and High Schools in this State.*

Passed July 11, 1851.

The People of the State of New-York, represented in Senate and Assembly, do enact as follows:

§ 1. It shall be lawful for an academy or high school for literary, scientific, charitable or religious purposes, to issue, create and possess a capital stock not exceeding ten thousand dollars, which stock shall be deemed personal property and shall be issued in shares of not less than ten dollars each to the several persons subscribing for and paying in the same; and in the election of trustees of any such corporation, each stockholder shall be entitled to give one vote upon each share of stock actually owned by him at the time of such election.

§ 2. Whenever any such corporation formed for the purpose of establishing an academy or high school shall have erected a building for school purposes of the value of two thousand dollars, and shall in all other respects comply with the conditions provided by law to authorise the regents to incorporate academies, said corporation shall be declared an academy by the regents of the University, and shall enjoy all the rights and privileges conferred by law on the academies of this State.

§ 3. This act shall take effect immediately.

CHAPTER 184. *An act relative to the incorporation of Colleges and Academies.*

Passed April 12, 1853.

The People of the State of New-York, represented in Senate and Assembly, do enact as follows:

§ 1. The regents of the University shall by general rules and regulations to be established by them from time to time, prescribe the requisites and conditions for the incorporation by them of any college, university, academy or other institution of learning, pursuant to the power vested in the said regents by the act entitled "An act relative to the University," passed April 5, 1813, and by the revised statutes of this State; the said regents are hereby empowered at any time by an instrument under their common seal, which shall be recorded in the office of the Secretary of State, to incorporate any university or college, or any academy, or other institution of learning, under such name, with such number of trustees or other managers, and with such powers and privileges and subject to such limitations and restrictions, in all respects as may be prescribed by law or as the said regents may deem proper in conformity thereto, and every institution so incorporated in addition to the powers which may be vested in them as aforesaid, shall have the general powers of a corporation under the revised statutes of this State.

§ 2. The said regents may at any time on sufficient cause shown and by an instrument under their common seal to be recorded as aforesaid, alter, amend or repeal the charter of any college, university, academy or other institution of learning which may hereafter be incorporated by them, and may, on the petition of any college, academy or other institution of learning in this State, now existing and subject, or which may hereafter become subject to their visitation, alter or modify the charter, and the rights, powers and privileges of such institution in such manner and on such terms and conditions as they may deem proper.

§ 3. The trustees of any academy possessing a capital stock pursuant to the act, chapter five hundred and forty-four of the laws of eighteen hundred and fifty-one, may by their by-laws prescribe the mode and manner of electing trustees of the said academy, and may make all necessary rules and regulations relative to such election; and the said trustees may, if they so determine, be divided into three classes as nearly equal as may be, who shall serve respectively one, two and three years, such terms of service to be determined by drawing therefor under the direction of the said trustees; and the trustees thereafter elected shall serve three years. The trustees may fill all vacancies according to their number by death, resignation, removal from the State or otherwise; and any election of trustees by any academy under said law heretofore held, is hereby affirmed and made valid, provided, that this act shall not affect any action heretofore arising out of any such election.

§ 4. The capital stock of any such academy shall not exceed fifty thousand dollars.

§ 5. Six members of the board of regents shall hereafter be necessary to form a quorum for the transaction of business.

§ 6. Any citizens not less than ten in number, of whom a majority shall be inhabitants of this State, who may desire to found or endow a medical or surgical college or school within this State, may make, sign and acknowledge before some officer authorised to take the acknowledgment of deeds, a certificate in writing, in which shall be stated the corporate name of the proposed institution, the names of the persons proposed for the first trustees, the plan on which, and the funds with which, it is intended to found and provide for said institution, and the name of the town or city in which it is proposed to locate the same; and shall file such certificate in the office of the Secretary of State, and transmit a duplicate thereof to the presiding officer of the regents of the University of the State of New-York.

§ 7. If it shall appear to the satisfaction of the regents of the University, that the sum of fifty thousand dollars has been subscribed in good faith for the endowment of such institution by the valid subscription of responsible parties, and at least two-thirds of that sum has been actually paid in or secured in such manner as the regents may approve, to be invested in buildings and site for college, museum, library, apparatus and other needful appurtenances of a medical college, or in bonds and mortgages on unincumbered real estate or stocks of the United States or of this State, they shall, by act under their seal, grant a charter pursuant to the provisions of this act, for the incorporation of such college, (naming therein as first trustees the persons specified in said certificate,) for a term of five years, with a condition or proviso therein that if within the said term of five years, the trustees of said college shall present to the regents satisfactory evidence that there has been paid in and invested as above prescribed, the whole of said sum of fifty thousand dollars, the charter thereof shall be made perpetual. Upon the fulfilment of said condition, or upon the payment in the first instance of the said sum of fifty thousand dollars, the said regents shall grant said college a perpetual charter.

§ 8. Such college may hold and possess real and personal property to the amount of two hundred thousand dollars, but the funds or property thereof shall not be used for any other purpose than for the legitimate business of such institution in the promotion of medical and surgical science and instruction in all departments of learning connected therewith.

§ 9. Such college shall be subject to the general provisions of the Revised Statutes, so far as the same are applicable, regulating the practice of physic and surgery within this State. It shall be subject to the visitation of the regents of the University, and shall make an annual report to them on oath, of the condition of said college and the various matters required by law to be reported by other colleges and academies, and of the investment of the funds of said college; and if at any time it shall appear that the sum required to be paid in has not been invested in the manner specified in the seventh section of this act, the regents of the university are hereby empowered to vacate and annul said charter.

§ 10. Every institution incorporated under this act shall have and possess all the powers and privileges, and be subject to the provisions, liabilities and restrictions of the eighteenth chapter of the first part of the revised statutes, so far as the same are applicable and have not been repealed. The board of trustees, which shall consist of not less than ten nor more than twenty-four persons, shall have power to make all needful by-laws and rules for the government and regulation of said college, the appointment of professors, instructors, and other officers thereof, the term of office and election of trustees, and so forth, not inconsistent with this act and the laws of this State. Such by-laws may be altered or amended by a vote of two-thirds of the members constituting said board, notice being given at a previous regular meeting of said board.

§ 11. The trustees for the time being of every college incorporated pursuant to this act, shall have power to grant and confer the degree of doctor of medicine upon the recommendation of the board of professors of said college and of at least three curators of the medical profession appointed by said trustees. But no person shall receive a diploma conferring such degree, unless he be of good moral character and of the age of twenty-one years, and shall have received a good English education, and shall have pursued the study of medicine and the sciences connected therewith for at least three years after the age of sixteen years, and have received instruction from some physician and surgeon fully qualified to practice his profession, until he is qualified to enter a medical college, and (except in cases hereafter provided,) shall also after that age have attended two complete courses of lectures delivered in some incorporated medical college.

§ 12. The board of trustees of every such college shall, upon payment of matriculation and demonstrator's fees (which shall not exceed the sum of five dollars each) admit to its course of instruction, without further charge, any number of young persons of the State of New-York, (not exceeding ten at any one time,) of good scholarship and moral character, who are in indigent circumstances; the evidence of qualification shall be a certificate from the judge of the county in which the applicant resides.

§ 13. This act shall take effect immediately, and all statutes and acts of the legislature inconsistent with the provisions of this act, are hereby repealed.

Chapter 433. *An act to provide for the establishment of Union Free Schools.*

Passed June 18, 1853; three-fifths being present.

The People of the State of New-York, represented in Senate and Assembly, do enact as follows:

§ 1. Whenever fifteen persons, entitled to vote at any meeting of the inhabitants of any school district in the State, shall sign a call for any such meeting, to be held for the purpose of determining, by a vote of such district, whether an union free school shall be established therein, in conformity with the provisions of this act, it shall be the duty of the trustees of such district, within ten days after such call shall have been presented to them, to give public notice that a meeting of the inhabitants of such district, entitled to vote thereat, will be held for such purpose as aforesaid, at the school house, or other more suitable place in such district, at a day and hour in such notice to be specified, not more than twenty days after the publication of such notice. The qualifications of such inhabitants entitled to vote at such meeting as now by law expressed, shall be sufficiently set forth in the notices aforesaid.

§ 2. The notices aforesaid, and at least five written or printed copies thereof, shall be severally posted at various conspicuous places in, and may also be published in any newspaper circulating within such districts. The trustees of any such district shall authorise and require any taxable inhabitant of the same to notify every inhabitant (qualified to vote as aforesaid) of such meeting, to be called as aforesaid, who shall give such notification, in the manner, and subject to the penalty, by law provided in the case of the formation of new school districts.

§ 3. The reasonable expense of such notices and of their publication and service shall be chargeable upon the district, in case an union free school is established therein under the provisions of this act, to be levied and collected upon and from the said district by the trustees as in cases of taxes now levied for school purposes; and if in the event such union free school shall not be established, then the said expense shall be chargeable upon the inhabitants signing the call, jointly and severally, to be sued for if necessary in any court having jurisdiction of the same.

§ 4. Whenever fifteen persons, entitled as aforesaid, from each of two or more adjoining districts, shall unite in a call for the consolidation of the same, and also for a meeting of the inhabitants entitled to vote, as aforesaid, in such districts, to determine whether an union free school shall be established within the limits of such districts, pursuant to the provisions of this act, it shall be the duty of the trustees of such districts, or a majority of them, to give like public notice of such meeting at some convenient place within such districts, and as central as may be, within the time and to be published in the manner set forth in the foregoing section, in each of said districts. The reasonable expenses of said notices and their service, in each of said districts, to be chargeable upon them in equal shares, or on the inhabitants signing the several calls therein, as by the foregoing section is provided.

§ 5. Any such meeting to be held as aforesaid, shall be organized by the appointment of a chairman and secretary, and may be adjourned from time to time if deemed by a majority vote expedient, provided any such adjournment shall not be for a longer period than ten days; and at any such meeting where at least one-third of such inhabitants of such district are present, whenever the question whether an union free school shall be established, in pursuance of the call for such meeting, shall be determined by a two-third vote of those present and entitled to vote, as aforesaid, in the affirmative, it shall then be lawful for such meeting to proceed to the election, by ballot, of not less than three nor more than nine trustees, who shall, by the order of such meeting, be divided into three several classes, the first class to hold for one, the second for two, and the third for three years: and thereupon the office of any existing board of trustees shall cease. The said trustees and their successors in office shall constitute a board of education of and for the city, village, district or districts for which they are elected, and the designation of the place whether as of such city, village or school district number   in the town of   or of consolidated school districts numbers   and   in the town of   shall be comprised in the title of said board, and the said board shall have the name and style of the board of education of   (adding the designation aforesaid.) Copies of the said call, minutes of said meeting or meetings, duly certified by the chairman and secretary thereof, shall be by them or either of them transmitted and deposited, one to and with the town clerk, one to and with the clerk of the county in which said districts are located, and one to and with the State superintendent: but when at any such meeting the questions as to the establishment of an union free school shall not be decided in the affirmative, as aforesaid, then all further proceedings at such meeting, except a motion to reconsider or adjourn, shall be dispensed with, and no such meeting shall be again called within one year thereafter.

§ 6. Whenever said board of education shall be constituted for any district or districts whose limits correspond with those of any incorporated village or city, the three classes shall hold jointly until the next charter election for such village or city, and their regular term of service as by the foregoing section shall be computed from the several days of such charter elections; and thereafter there shall be annually elected in such villages and cities, in the same manner as and upon the same ticket with the charter officers thereof, trustees of the said union free schools, to supply the places of those whose term by the classification aforesaid are about to expire. The term of office of all trustees elected under the provisions of this act, after the first election as aforesaid, shall be three years.

§ 7. The said boards of education are hereby severally created bodies corporate; and each shall, at their first meeting, and at the times thereafter fixed by their by-laws as for their annual meetings, elect one of their number president, another the clerk thereof, the latter of whom shall also be the general librarian for the district. In districts other than those whose limits correspond with those of any city or incorporated village, said board shall have power to appoint one of the taxable inhabitants of their district, treasurer, and another, collector of the moneys raised and to be raised within the same for school purposes, who shall severally hold such appointments for one year from the date thereof, and until others are appointed in their stead, unless sooner removed by the board for cause. Such treasurer and collector shall severally, and within ten days after notice of their appointment in writing duly served upon them, and before entering upon the duties of their offices, execute and deliver to the said board of education a bond, with such sufficient penalty and sureties as the board may require, conditioned for the faithful discharge of the duties of their respective offices; and in case such bond shall not be given within the time specified, such offices shall thereby become vacant, and said board shall thereupon make other appointments to supply such vacancies.

§ 8. The corporate authorities of any incorporated village or city in which any such union free school shall be established, shall have power, and it shall be their duty, to raise from time to time by tax to be levied upon all the real and personal property in said cities and villages respectively, as by law provided for the defraying of the expenses of their respective municipal governments, such sum or sums as the board of education established therein shall declare necessary (in a detailed statement to be furnished in writing by the said board to such municipal authorities, of each and every expenditure so declared to be necessary) for the furtherance of any of the powers vested in them by law; provided, however, that the said corporate authorities shall have power to refuse for one year any supplies other than those for the annual support of the teachers of said union free schools, and the necessary contingent expenses of the said schools. And in case the said corporate authorities shall refuse as aforesaid, they shall communicate in writing to the said board of education their objections to each and every expenditure which they may, under the power as aforesaid, refuse to allow; and thereupon the said board of education shall cause the said communication to be published six times in at least one paper circulating in said village or city. Nothing in this section contained shall be construed to prohibit any such municipal government of any city or village from reconsidering their vote in regard to the refusal of any such supplies as aforesaid, within the year above specified.

§ 9. The taxable inhabitants of any districts, as aforesaid, other than those whose limits correspond with those of any city or incorporated village, at any annual or special meeting, held as by provisions of existing law, may vote to authorise such acts and raise such sums of money as they shall deem expedient for the purpose of making additions, alterations or improvements, with reference to site or structures, in the academy or union free school buildings, or of buying apparatus or fixtures, or for such other purpose as they may by a two-third vote approve; and to direct the trustees to cause the sums voted to be levied and raised by instalments or directly by a tax; and such trustees shall make out a tax list, in the manner provided by law in cases of school district taxes, and direct such taxes or such instalments to be collected at the times they shall become due. And the inhabitants of such districts shall have no power to rescind the vote to raise such money or to reduce the amount at any subsequent meeting, unless the same be done within ten days after the same shall have been first voted.

§ 10. Whenever any school districts shall have been consolidated as aforesaid, or by any provision of law, they shall be entitled to the same portion of the one-third of the public moneys, distributed among the several school districts in pursuance of an act entitled "An act to establish free schools throughout the State," passed April 12, 1851, as they would have been entitled to if they had not been consolidated; provided that they shall not receive such portions for any longer period than for five years after the passage of this act, in the cases of all districts already consolidated; and in other cases, for five years after such consolidation shall have been effected, as aforesaid.

§ 11. The said boards of education, by this act established, shall severally have power:

1. To pass such by-laws as they may deem proper for the regulation and exercise of their lawful business and powers.

2. To fill any vacancy which may happen in said board, by reason of the death, removal or refusal to serve of any member or officer of said board; and the person so appointed in the place of

any such member of the board, shall hold his office until the next election of trustees, as by this act provided.

3. To remove any member of their board for official misconduct. But a written copy of all charges made of such misconduct shall be served upon him at least ten days before the time appointed for a hearing of the same; and he shall be allowed a full and fair opportunity to refute such charges before removal.

4. To take charge and possession of the school houses, sites, lots, furniture, books, apparatus, and all school property within their respective districts, and the title of the same shall be vested respectively in said boards of education, and the same shall not be subject to taxation for any purpose.

5. To take and hold, and for the use of the said schools or of any department of the same, any real estate transferred to it by gift, grant, bequest or devise, or any gift, legacy or annuity, of whatever kind, given or bequeathed to the said board, and apply the same, or the interest or proceeds thereof, according to the instructions of the donor or testator.

6. To have in all respects the superintendence, management and control of said union free schools, and to establish in the same an academical department, whenever in their judgments the same is warranted by the demand for such instruction; to receive into such union free schools any pupils residing out of said districts, and to regulate and establish the tuition fees of such non-resident pupils in the several departments of said schools, and also those of scholars residing in said districts and attending its academical department; to regulate, in accordance with the provisions of this act, the transfer of scholars from the primary to the academical departments, and from class to class as their degree of scholarship may warrant; to direct what text books shall be used therein; to provide fuel, furniture, apparatus and other necessaries for the use of said schools, and to appoint such assistant librarians as they may, from time to time, deem necessary.

7. To contract with, license and employ teachers competent in the several departments of instruction, in all not less than one for every sixty scholars attending such schools, to remove them at any time for neglect of duty or immoral conduct, and to pay the wages of such teachers out of the moneys appropriated for that purpose.

8. And generally to possess all the powers and privileges and be subject to all the duties in respect to the common schools, or the common school departments in any union free school in said districts, which the trustees of common schools now possess or are subject to, not inconsistent with the provisions of this act, and to enjoy, whenever an academical department shall be by them established, all the immunities and privileges now enjoyed by the academies of this State.

§ 12. It shall be the duty of each of the said boards of education to have a regular meeting at least once in each quarter, and at such meetings to appoint one or more committees, each to consist of not less than two of their own number, to visit every school or department under the supervision of said board, and such committees shall visit all said schools at least twice in each quarter, and report at the next regular meeting of the board on the condition and prospects thereof.

§ 13. It shall also be the duty of said boards, respectively, to have reference in all their expenditures and contracts to the amount of moneys which shall be appropriated, or subject to their order or drafts, during the current year, and not to exceed that amount. And said boards shall severally apply all the public moneys apportioned to the common school districts under their charge to the departments below the academical; and all moneys from that of the literature fund, or otherwise, appropriated for the support of the academical departments, to the latter departments.

§ 14. All moneys raised for the use of the union free schools in any city or incorporated village, or apportioned to the same from the income of the literature, common school or United States deposit funds, or otherwise, shall be paid into the treasury of such city or village, to the credit of the board of education therein; and the funds so received into such treasury shall be kept separate and distinct from any other funds received into the said treasury. And the officer having the charge thereof shall give such additional security for the safe custody thereof as the corporate authorities of such city or village shall require. No money shall be drawn from such funds, credited to the several boards of education, unless in pursuance of a resolution or resolutions of said board, and on drafts drawn by the president and countersigned by the secretary, payable to the order of the person or persons entitled to receive such money, and stating on their face the purpose or service for which such moneys have been authorised to be paid by the said board of education.

§ 15. All moneys raised for the use of said union free schools, other than those whose limits correspond with those of any cities and incorporated villages, or apportioned from the income of the literature or common school or United States deposit funds, or otherwise, shall be paid to the respective treasurers of the said several boards of education entitled to receive the same, and be by them applied to the uses of said several boards, who shall annually render their accounts of all moneys received and expended by them for the use of said schools, with every voucher for the same, and certified copies of all orders of the said boards touching the same to the town superintendents of the town in which said districts are severally located.

§ 16. Every academical department so to be established, as aforesaid, shall be under the visitation of the regents of the university, and shall be subject in its course of education and matters pertaining thereto (but not in reference to the buildings or erections in which the same is held, unless in cases where the buildings aforesaid are separate from those of the common school department) to all the regulations made in regard to academies by the said regents. In such departments, the qualifications for the entrance of any pupil shall be the same as those established by the said regents for admission into any academy of the State under their supervision.

§ 17. Whenever an union school shall be established under the provisions of this act, and there shall exist within its district an academy, the trustees thereof may, by an unanimous vote, to be attested by their signatures and filed in the office of the clerk of the county, declare their offices vacant; and thereafter the trustees of such union school, shall become the trustees of the said academy, and be charged with all the duties of the former trustees, and the said academy shall be regarded as the academical department of such union school.

§ 18. All acts or parts of acts inconsistent with the provisions aforesaid are hereby repealed; and the provisions of this act, in reference to the establishment of academical departments, shall be as applicable to those school districts or villages where free schools have been established, by special charter, as if no such charter had been granted; but nothing in this act shall be construed to impair the charters or alter or abridge the rights or privileges of any free schools now by law established in any city of the State.

§ 19. This act shall take effect immediately.

II. Of the Incorporation of Academies.

I. *The applicants for the incorporation of an academy should consult article third of the Revised Statutes, as printed on page* 17, *and the law of* 1838, *as given in the Revised Statutes, section* 32. *See page* 13.

II. *Ordinance of the Regents, passed April* 6, 1849.

No application for the incorporation of an academy will be granted, nor will any academy be received under the visitation of the Regents, so as to entitle it to share in the distribution of the funds granted to academies, unless it appears that the academy lot and building and the library and philosophical apparatus which it may own have been fully paid for.

The Regents have felt themselves obliged to adopt this ordinance from the fact that a number of academies which had shared in the distribution of the literature funds for several years, have become insolvent in consequence of some lien on their property most generally existing from the outset of their enterprise, and which constantly embarrassed them in their operations. The requisitions for obtaining a charter are so reasonable, that with a vigorous and proper effort any community actually needing an academy, can readily raise the full amount required for that purpose.

In consequence of the passage of the law to incorporate academies and high schools in this State, chap. 544, Session Laws of 1851, a modification of the above ordinance became necessary. The following is therefore now in force:

III. *Ordinance of the Regents, passed October* 14, 1851.

No academy will be received under the visitation of the Regents, so as to entitle it to share in the distribution of the funds granted to academies, unless it appears that the academy lot and buildings, and the library and philosophical apparatus which it may own, have been fully paid for. Nor will the Regents incorporate any academy, unless it appears in like manner that the academy lot and buildings, and the library and philosophical apparatus, have been fully paid for, unless, under peculiar circumstances, justifying in their judgment a departure from this rule; and in any such case, the application will be granted only on the condition, to be inserted in the charter, that the academy so incorporated shall not be entitled to share in the distribution of the fund granted to academies, until its debts have been fully paid.

IV. *Form of an application for the incorporation of an Academy by the Regents of the University.*

To the Regents of the University of the State of New-York:

The application of the subscribers, inhabitants of &c., respectfully represents, That being desirous to found an academy at &c., they have, for that purpose, (together with others, if the fact be so,) procured a suitable lot, erected a suitable building thereon, and supplied it with a suitable library and apparatus, for the accommodation of such academy, as will appear by the following description.

1. *Ground for Academy Buildings.*

The lot of ground on which the buildings of said academy stand, or which is to be used for its accommodation, consists of [here state the quantity, either in acres or parts of acres, or the number of feet in breadth and depth.] The lot of ground was purchased in the year , for $; or it was given to the academy in the year [as the case may be.] There was then no improvements on it, [or if there were any, describe them ;] state the title to the ground, whether in perpetuity, or for a term of years, and if it be subject to a ground rent, state amount, &c. Give a general description of all improvements (except buildings) made on it. After giving all such and similar data on which estimates of value depend, state the present value of the ground, including fences, ornamental trees, and all other improvements, except buildings.

2. *Academy Buildings.*

The buildings erected on the ground above described, and to be used for the accommodation of the academy, consist of [here describe the principal buildings, with their dimensions; state when and of what materials they were originally built, or have been since enlarged or improved; give a general description of their internal divisions, fitness or convenience for use, &c., with a statement of the original or first cost of the buildings, and of all additions or improvements thereto, so far as the same can be ascertained. Then state their present condition as to their being in or out of repair, and if out of repair, what will be the probable cost of putting them in good repair. After giving all such and similar data on which estimates of value depend, state the present actual value of such buildings.]

3. *Academy Library.*

The following is a catalogue of all the books belonging to said proposed academy, with the original or first cost, (so far as it can be ascertained,) and the present value of each book, [proceed with the catalogue in the following form.]

Title or name of books arranged according to catalogue, if any, in use.	Number of volumes.	Original cost.	Present value.
[Give the total of each column.]			

Give a general description of the condition of the books in the library in respect to their being new or old, in good order or worn out, &c.

4. *Philosophical Apparatus.*

The following is an inventory of all the articles of philosophical or other apparatus at the date of this application, with the original or first cost, (so far as can be ascertained,) and the present value of each article, [here proceed with the inventory, including in it, besides what is strictly and technically philosophical apparatus, all instruments used in, or illustrative of any of the arts or sciences.]

Description or name of each article.	Original cost.	Present value.

State the totals, and give a general description of the condition of the apparatus in respect to its being new or old, in good order or injured, &c.

5. *Title of property, Incumbrances, &c.*

The evidences of title to the property described in the preceding sections of this report, have been submitted to of, &c., who is a counsellor at law in the supreme court, whose certificate in writing, as to the nature and validity of said title, accompanies this report.* The said property is free from all incumbrances, if such be the case; [or if there be any incumbrances on it, state the general amount of them, and refer to certificate of said counsel for particulars, &c.]

6. *Other Academic Property.*

The property of the proposed academy, other than the academy lot, buildings, library and apparatus above described, consists of, [here describe the property in the most general terms, such as the following :]

Bonds and mortgages, considered good,............. $
A house and lot at, &c., worth,....................
100 acres of wild land, &c., ...

Total,................................ .... $

7. *Summary statements.*

The total value of all the academic property above described, is as follows :

Value of lot for academy buildings,................. $
Value of buildings thereon,.........................
Value of library,...................................
Value of philosophical apparatus, ...

Total value of lot, buildings, library and apparatus, $
Deduct for incumbrances, if any, thereon, ...
Balance of value over and above all incumbrances,...
Add for other academic property, ...

Total value of the whole, ... $

8. *Debts.*

The debts contracted on account of the academy now asked to be incorporated, and which remain unpaid at the date of this application, amount to $

* The certificate of counsel must state that he "has caused the ordinary searches to be made for incumbrances." For more specific directions, see Ordinance of October 20, 1853, (hereafter published.) "That it shall be the duty of the trustees of every such academy, previous to making their first report or application required by this ordinance, to submit the evidences of their title to the ground occupied for their academic buildings, to some person of the degree of counsellor at law in the supreme court, for his examination and to obtain from him a certificate in writing, stating his examination of the title submitted to him, with his opinion as to the nature and validity of such title, and stating, also, that he has caused the ordinary searches to be made for incumbrances on such property, with the result of such searches; which said certificate shall be transmitted by the said trustees, together with their said first report or application, to the said Regents."

And the said subscribers further represent, that they have contributed more than one-half in value of the property collected for the use of said academy, as herein before set forth; that they are desirous to have the said academy incorporated, by the name of [here state the name, which it is desirable should be descriptive of the place where the academy is;] and to that end they hereby nominate tho following named persons to be the first trustees of said academy: [here insert names—but there cannot be more than 24 nor less than 12 trustees.]

The said subscribers do therefore hereby make application to the Regents of the University for the incorporation of the persons above nominated as the first trustees of said academy by the name above specified. (Here follow the signatures of the subscribers.)*

Authentication of Application.

The preceding application was submitted to a meeting of the subscribers held by them on the day of at which meeting the following named persons were present, [state names,] and having been read and approved, it was duly adopted as the application of said meeting, and ordered (after being verified by the oath of the chairman or presiding officer) to be transmitted to the Regents of the University, pursuant to their ordinance in such case made and provided.

All of which is hereby done in obedience to said order this day of

A. B., *Chairman or Presiding Officer.*

Affidavit above referred to.

County of *ss.*—A. B. being duly sworn (or affirmed, as the case may be,) deposeth and saith, that he was the chairman or presiding officer of the meeting, held as above stated, of contributors to the proposed academy, asking for an incorporation by the name of academy; that he is acquainted with the contents of said application, and that the statement of facts therein set forth is in all respects true to the best of his knowledge, information and belief.

A. B.

Sworn before me this day of

* It has happened that the signatures of the subscribers as above, are all *in the same handwriting!* This is manifestly incorrect, and will undoubtedly endanger the success of an application.

V. *Form of an Application of an Academy already incorporated by the Legislature, to become subject to the visitation of the Regents.*

The introductory part of the report should in this case be as follows:

The trustees of academy, established at respectfully represent that they were incorporated by the legislature on the day of A. D. 18 ; that they are desirous to become subject to the visitation of the Regents of the University, to enable them to participate in the distribution of the moneys belonging to the Literature Fund, pursuant to the statute in such case made and provided; and to that end they hereby subject the said academy to the visitation of the said Regents, to the same extent and in the same manner as if they had been originally incorporated by them; and the said trustees herewith submit the following statement of the condition of their institution on the date of this application, in respect to the several subject matters required to be embraced in it.

[Here adopt the form given in pages 47–50, as follows :]

1. *Ground for Academy Buildings.*

The only alteration necessary is to strike out the words "to be" in the second line.

2. *Academy Buildings.*

The same alteration in line 1.

3. *Academy Library.*

Say, The following is a catalogue of all the books *belonging to said Academy at the date of this report*, with, &c.

4. *Philosophical Apparatus.*

Say, The following is an inventory of all the articles of philosophical or other apparatus *belonging to said Academy at the date of this report*, with, &c.

5. *Title to Property, Incumbrances, &c.*

Say, The evidences of the title of *the said Academy*, to the property, &c.

6. *Other Academic property.*

Say, The property of the *Academy*, other, &c.

7. *Summary Statements.*

8. *Debts.*

The debts contracted by the academy which remained unpaid on the said day of &c., including all arrears of interest, (if any) and all outstanding or unpaid accounts acknowledged as debts, amounted on that day to $ (The amount of incumbrances on the academic property should be included in this sum.)*

Add

9. *Departments.*

The departments of instruction established and in practical operation in the academy, are [here describe the different departments, if there be more than one, by reference to the subjects of instruction in each, or to the sex of the scholars attending it, and in all cases state whether male and female scholars are in the same or different departments.]

[*Memorandum.*—It will be readily understood, after the above directions, that all the variations in these forms are owing to the fact that in one case there is an application for an incorporation, and in the other the academy is already incorporated. It is necessary to use terms conformable to the respective cases.]

10. *Conclusion and Authentication of Report.*

The preceding report from academy was submitted to the trustees of said academy, at a meeting legally held by them on the day of, &c., at which meeting the following named trustees were present, [state names,] and having been read and approved, it was duly adopted at said meeting as the report of said academy, and ordered (after being verified by the oath of the presiding officer at said meeting and recorded on the minutes of its proceedings,†) to be transmitted to the Regents of the University pursuant to the provisions of their ordinance in such case made and provided.

All which is hereby done in obedience to said order this day of, &c. *A. B., President, or President pro tem.*
(*as the case may be*)
of Academy.

11. *Affidavit above referred to.*

County of *ss.*—A. B. being duly sworn or affirmed (as the case may be,) deposeth and saith, that he is one of the trustees of academy, (whose report to the Regents of the University immediately precedes this affidavit,) that he officiated as the presiding officer at the meeting of the trustees of said academy referred to in the concluding part of said report—that he is acquainted with the contents of said report—that said report is made in the form required by the latest instructions received from the Regents of the University, and that the statement of facts therein set forth is in all respects true according to the best of his knowledge, information and belief. A. B.

Sworn before me this day of, &c.

* A certificate of counsel as to the title, and that he has "caused the ordinary searches for incumbrances to be made," is here also required. See page 49.

† It is proper to have the trustees' part of every report entered on their minutes—as it is an important part of their proceedings, and a record or copy of it will be required for reference in making future reports.

VI. NOTES.

The requirements necessary to enable an academy to participate in the annual distribution of the Literature Fund, may be summed up as follows.

1. The erection of a proper building and suitable and necessary accommodations for the scholars.

2. That such academy is furnished with a library and philosophical apparatus.

In answer to the enquiry as to what shall be deemed a *suitable* library and apparatus, the following resolution of the Regents, passed June 7, 1829, is subjoined.

Resolved, That no academy shall hereafter be allowed to participate in the distribution of the Literature Fund, unless it shall have, at the time of making its annual report next preceding every such distribution, a library of the value of at least $150, and a philosophical and chemical apparatus of at least the value of $150.

Is it absolutely necessary, when the incorporation of an academy is asked for, that said academy should have a library and apparatus respectively of the value of $150?

In answer to this, the Regents have made the following decisions:

A. That the mere subscription of three hundred dollars for the purchase of a library and apparatus is not a sufficient compliance with the law. [Minutes of February 16, 1841.]

B. That there must be some articles of each actually purchased, before they will incorporate an academy. [Minutes of April 18, 1845.]

C. That they will not insist upon, although they prefer a library and apparatus to the full amount specified above, as preliminary to the incorporation of an academy; *it being understood that said academy cannot receive any portion of the income of the Literature Fund, until it reports a library and apparatus of the full value.**—*Ibid.*

3. That a proper preceptor has been and is employed for the instruction of the pupils of such academy.

4. That said building, library and apparatus are sufficient for the purpose intended, and the whole is of the value of at least twenty-five hundred dollars.†

5. It may happen, that an incorporated academy, applying to become subject to the visitation of the Regents, is at the date of that application prepared to show that it has instructed students in classical studies, or students in the higher branches of English education for four months, so as to entitle it to a distributive share of the Literature Fund. Should this be desired, it will be proper to send another report, according to the form hereafter given for annual reports; but it will not be necessary to repeat the second time the subjects already noticed in the application, except by referring to them. The other heads should be filled up, and the teacher's report annexed, as hereafter directed.

* A list of books and apparatus *recommended* by the Regents to be purchased, will be found in subsequent pages.

† It must be understood, although the value of the academy building *alone* is $2,500, and even upwards, yet the academy is still required to provide itself with a library and apparatus, to the amount above stated.

6. The same rule has been extended to *applicants for an incorporation by the Regents,* they shewing that while their building (for example) was erecting, the system of required instruction was carried on in a temporary building, &c., &c.

VII. *Charter of an Academy incorporated by the Regents.*

The charter is prepared and executed by the officers of the Regents of the University. It is then forwarded to the office of the Secretary of State in order that both it and the application on which it was granted, may be recorded. This is always done within a reasonable time after the charter has passed, and *applicatian should accordingly be made directly to the Secretary's office for it.*

Fees are required to be paid for recording the above instruments, generally from $3 to $5.

VIII. *Notice to Academies incorporated prior to* 1838.

Previous to the passage of the Act of the 17th of April, 1838, *the following resolution of the Regents of the University, relative to the incorporation of Academies (passed originally in* 1801) *was in force.*

Resolved, That in future no academy ought to be incorporated, unless it shall be made to appear by satisfactory evidence to this board, that a proper building for the purpose hath been erected, and finished and paid for; and that funds have been obtained and well secured, producing an annual net income of at least $100, (increased in 1815 to $250;) and further, that there be a condition in the charter of incorporation, that the principal or estate producing said income shall never be diminished or appropriated, and that the said income shall be applied only to the maintenance or salary of the professors or tutors of the academy.

This is now of course abrogated, and the provisions of the act of April 17, 1838, are in full and exclusive force. See an ordinance of the Regents, passed October 20, 1853, hereafter published.

In all future applications to the Regents of the University for the incorporation of academies, *the applicants will be required to shew property, in buildings, library and apparatus, to the value of* $2,500, without regard to other kinds of property, or to annual revenue.

There are academies whose charter contains the provisions of the ordinance of 1801, and it has been enquired whether the investments there required must be continued, under the present regulations. In answer to this, is subjoined an extract from a report made to the Regents on a petition of Clarkson Academy, by a committee of which Mr. McKown was chairman, Feb. 28, 1845, and unanimously approved by them.

"It may perhaps be proper for the committee to add, that they are not aware of any obstacle to prevent the trustees of Clarkson Academy, if they deem fit and are clothed with authority for that purpose, by the stockholders, to divest themselves of their permanent fund and yet remain under the visitation of the Regents and be entitled to share in the distribution of the Literature Fund, provided they continue to have a suitable library, building and apparatus, of the value of at least $2,500, according to the act of 1838."

IX. *Form of an application for the incorporation of an Academy with a capital stock, pursuant to chapter* 544 *of the Laws of* 1851, *and chapter* 184 *of the Laws of* 1853.

The Regents of the University having decided to grant charters, on certain conditions, to Academies founded on a capital stock, pursuant to the provisions of the laws above recited, they have prescribed the following:

FORM OF AN APPLICATION.

To the Regents of the University of the State of New-York:

The petition of the undersigned, inhabitants of the in the county of

Respectfully represents:

That they are desirous to found an Academy in the in the county of with a capital stock of dollars, to be divided into shares of dollars* each, pursuant to the act, chapter 544 of the Laws of 1851, and the act, chapter 184 of the Laws of 1853, and that subscriptions to the said capital stock have been procured to the amount of dollars, as will appear by the list of said subscriptions, a copy whereof is hereto annexed, and from which it also appears that your petitioners are the subscribers for more than one half of the said amount. That at least ten per cent of the amount subscribed has been paid by or for each subscriber in cash, and is now held by your petitioners on their behalf, for the purposes of the incorporation herein prayed for. That all the said subscriptions are, as your petitioners believe, made in good faith and by parties who have the ability to pay the amount subscribed by them respectively. That your petitioners are desirous that the said academy may be incorporated by the name of and that they do hereby nominate the following persons as the first trustees thereof.†

The undersigned do therefore request the Regents to incorporate the persons above nominated as the first trustees of the said Academy by the name above mentioned. It being distinctly declared and understood by your petitioners that the said incorporation is now asked for to facilitate the purchase of a site for the said Academy and the erection of the necessary buildings therefor, and for the commencement and organization of a proper course of instruction therein; and that if a proper building for the purposes of the said Academy shall not be provided and erected, and a suitable course of instruction be organised within two years from the granting of the charter prayed for, and a report of the same made by the said trustees or

* The shares cannot be less than ten dollars each.

† The trustees should not be less than nine, nor more than twenty-one in number.

their successors to the said Regents, containing all the particulars required in the case of an application for granting a charter to an Academy already endowed with sufficient academic property, (see page 47, No. 4, Form of an application for the incorporation of an Academy by the Regents of the University,) that then, at any time thereafter, the said charter, on a declaration to that effect to be made by the said Regents, on their minutes, on evidence satisfactory to them, shall become and be absolutely void; and on the further understanding, that the said Academy is not to be entitled to any part of the funds which may by law, from time to time, be distributed to or divided among the incorporated Academies of the State, arising from the income of the Literature Fund or otherwise, until the said capital stock shall have been fully paid in, and until a suitable Academy building shall have been erected or procured therefor, and a library and philosophical apparatus obtained of the character andvalue required by the ordinances of the Regents.

AFFIDAVIT.

County of ss:

A, B, C, signers to the above application, being duly sworn, (or affirmed, as the case may be) depose and say, that they are acquainted with the contents of the preceding application, and that the statement of facts therein set forth, is in all respects true, to the best of their knowledge, information and belief, that they believe the said subscription to be a valid one, and that the application is made in good faith for the purposes therein stated. (Signed,) A.

B.

Sworn before me, } C.
this day of }

[Here add a copy of the subscription list.]

X. Form of an application for the incorporation of an Academy to be founded on donations or endowments, not in the form of a capital stock, on certain conditions.

The Regents of the University having decided, on certain conditions, to grant charters to academies founded on donations or endowments, not in the form of capital stock, have prescribed for the same, the following:

FORM OF APPLICATION.

To the Regents of the University of the State of New-York:

The petition of the undersigned, inhabitants of the   in the county of

Respectfully represents:

That they are desirous to found an academy in the   in the county of   and that for the endowment of such Academy, subscriptions have been obtained to the amount of   dollars,* as will appear by a copy of the subscription list hereunto annexed, and from which it also appears that your petitioners have contributed more than one half of the said amount thus subscribed. That at least ten per cent of the amount subscribed has been paid by or for each subscriber in cash, and is now held by your petitioners or on their behalf, for the purposes of the incorporation herein prayed for. That all the said subscriptions are, as your petitioners believe, made in good faith and by parties who have the ability to pay the amount subscribed by them respectively, and that no other property has been contributed or collected for the said academy. That your petitioners request that the said academy may be incorporated by the name of   and they do hereby nominate the following persons as the first trustees thereof:

The undersigned do therefore request the Regents to incorporate the persons above nominated as the first trustees of the said academy by the name above mentioned. It being distinctly declared and understood by your petitioners that the said incorporation is now asked for to facilitate the purchase of a site for the said academy and the erection of the necessary buildings therefor, and for the commencement and organization of a proper course of instruction therein; and that if a proper building for the purposes of the said academy shall not be provided or erected, and a suitable course of instruction be organized within two years from the granting of the charter prayed for, and a report of the same be

* Subscriptions must amount to at least $2500.

made by the said trustees to the said Regents, containing all the particulars required in the case of an application for the incorporation of an academy by the said Regents, (see pages 47–51 of these instructions, form numbered 4,) that then at any time thereafter, the said charter, on a declaration to that effect to be made by the said Regents on their minutes, on evidence satisfactory to them, shall become and be absolutely void; and on the further understanding, that the said academy is not to be entitled to any part of the funds which may by law, from time to time, be distributed to or divided among the incorporated academies of the State, arising from the income of the Literature Fund or otherwise, until at least two thousand five hundred dollars shall have been paid in or contributed towards founding and establishing the same, and until a suitable academy building shall have been erected or procured therefor, and a library and philosophical apparatus obtained of the character and value required by the ordinances of the Regents. (Here subjoin the signatures of the petitioners who have contributed as above.)

AFFIDAVIT.

County of ss:

A, B, C, (three at least) signers of the above application, being duly sworn, (or affirmed as the case may be) depose and say, that they are acquainted with the contents of the previous application, and that the statement of facts therein set forth, is in all respects true, to the best of their knowledge, information and belief; that they believe the said subscription to be a valid one, and that the application is made in good faith for the purposes therein stated. (Signed,) A.

B.

C.

Sworn before me }
this day of }

[Here add a copy of the subscription list.]

(If any donations, other than in money, have been made to the academy, such as a lot for the site of the building, &c. &c., the fact should be stated in the application, and the property described, and the value thereof, and the foregoing should be altered to conform to the circumstances.)

III. Of the Annual Reports of Academies.

I. LAWS OF THE STATE.

[See pages 14, 15.]

II. ORDINANCE OF THE REGENTS OF THE UNIVERSITY.

Ordinance of the Regents of the University, prescribing the requisites and forms of application, and of the annual reports of Academies, and defining classical studies and the higher branches of English education pursued in the same, passed October 20, 1853.**

1. *The Regents, desirous of consolidating all their ordinances and resolutions on the above subjects, contained in their several ordinances of the date of March* 18, 1828, *April* 25, 1838, *and April* 5, 1849, *and their respective resolutions of February* 26, 1834, *April* 11, 1843, *February* 27, 1844, *and June* 1, 1844, *(all of which appear in the "Instructions of the Regents of the University," published in* 1849,) *and also of adding thereto some important provisions, do ordain and declare that the present ordinance shall be in force from and after the* 1*st May,* 1854, *and all ordinances or parts thereof, and resolutions inconsistent with the same, shall be of no force or effect after the above date.*

AS TO THE FINANCIAL CONDITION OF ACADEMIES.

SECTION 1. Every application to the Regents of the University for an absolute charter for the incorporation of an academy founded on the endowment of property already possessed by the applicants, and every application of an academy, incorporated by the Legislature, to become subject to the visitation of the Regents, shall set forth, with all practicable precision, and in such form as is or shall be prescribed by the Regents, a particular statement showing

1st. The extent, general description, title, and value of the ground on which their academy edifice shall be erected, or which shall be used for its accommodation at the time of making such application.

** The important alterations made from former ordinances, are, for convenience, put in italics. The Regents have been induced to require that the age of students claimed, shall be TWELVE YEARS, (see section 10) from an impression that this change is imperatively required, both from the higher standing of academies, and from the rapid improvement of common schools. The provision as to TEN YEARS of age was made in 1834; and, certainly, the progress of twenty years demands the present alteration. Again as to section 7, the Regents have ascertained that in some academies subject to their visitation, students are allowed to commence and pursue classical studies, with a view to their becoming classical scholars, within the meaning of this ordinance, without being required to attain the same degree of proficiency in English studies as is required of students in the higher branches of English education, as a prerequisite of their becoming students within the meaning of this ordinance. The Regents are of opinion that both classes of such students should be required to pursue the like preliminary studies.

Sec. 6. The text books are changed to conform to present usage.

2d. The dimensions, general description, and value of the build ings erected on such ground for the use or accommodation of such academy, at the time last aforesaid.

3d. An inventory or catalogue of all the books and articles of philosophical or other apparatus belonging to such academy, with a just and fair estimate of their value, at the time last above referred to.

4th. A particular statement of all incumbrances on such academic property, or on any part thereof, at the time last above mentioned—it being the intention of the Regents to require every academy subject to their visitation, to own and possess such property to the value of at least two thousand five hundred dollars, over and above all incumbrances thereon, as a condition on which such academy will be allowed to receive a distributive share of the moneys belonging to the Literature Fund.*

And to the end that the Regents may be the better enabled to ascertain the true value of such academic grounds, buildings and apparatus, at the time of making such application, the said statements shall also set forth and show, when and how the title to such ground,† library and apparatus was first acquired, and if acquired by purchase, what the original or first cost thereof was; and also, when such buildings were erected, enlarged or otherwise improved, of what materials they are constructed, with the original or first cost of such buildings or improvements; also, the state or condition of such academic property, at the time of making such report or application, in respect to its repair or fitness for use; and if the same be not in good repair, wherein, and how long it has been out of repair, and the probable cost of putting it in good repair, together with such other matters as may be found to influence in any respect the value of such property. That it shall be the duty of the trustees of every such academy, previous to making their said application as required by this ordinance, to submit the evidences of their title to the ground occupied for their academic buildings, to some person of the degree of counsellor at law in the supreme court, for his examination and to obtain from him a certificate in writing, stating his examination of the title submitted to him, with his opinion as to the nature and validity of such title, and stating, also, that he has caused the ordinary searches to be made for incumbrances on such property, with the result of such searches; which said certificate shall be transmitted by the said trustees, together with their said application, to the said Regents.

§ 2. The trustees of every academy incorporated by the Regents or subject to their visitation, shall, in every annual report to the Regents, either make and transmit a full statement of all the academic property then belonging to them in the manner re-

* See ordinances of the Regents in relation to academic debts on page 46, which are still in force.

† Forms of application, in conformity to the above section, are given at pages 47 and 51.

quired by the first section of this ordinance, or in lieu thereof, state whether such property remains in all respects the same as at the time of making any previous statement thereof, to be particularly referred to by them, or whether the same has been increased or diminished in quantity, enhanced or depreciated in value, and to what extent, or has in any other and what respect, undergone any and what change, since the time of making such previous statement—showing in all cases the true value of such property at the time of making such report as aforesaid; and it is hereby made the duty of the trustees of every such academy, at some time during the year ending on the date of every such report, to cause all the books and articles of apparatus then actually possessed by them, to be compared with the original catalogues or inventories thereof, (to be always preserved for that purpose,) to ascertain whether any of their books or articles of apparatus shall have been lost, destroyed or damaged beyond the ordinary wear and tear thereof from necessary use, and to state in every such report whether such duty has been discharged, and whether any, and if any, what part of their books and apparatus shall on such comparison be found to be lost, destroyed or damaged as aforesaid, and through whose act, omission or neglect such loss or damage shall have happened.

§ 3. Every academy subject to the visitation of the Regents of the University, and claiming a distributive share of the income of the Literature Fund, shall annually on or before the first day of February, make and transmit to the Regents, (so that the same may be received by their secretary on or before that day,) a report in writing, in such form as is or shall be prescribed by the Regents, exhibiting a full view of its state and condition, at the time referred to in its report, in respect to the following particulars, viz:

Condition and value of its academic lot and buildings:

Condition and value of its library and philosophical apparatus:

Kind and value of its other property:

Incumbrances and debts:

Annual revenue and expenditures:

Amount of money received by it from the Regents of the University since its last annual report, and how the same shall have been expended:

And also in respect to all such other matters as shall be required by the said Regents to be reported on in the form prescribed by them as aforesaid.

AS TO THE LITERARY AND SCIENTIFIC CONDITION OF ACADEMIES.

§ 4. The report required as above, shall also contain the number and names of its teachers, and the annual salary or compensation allowed to each; the age of such teachers, the time he or she has been engaged in teaching; the general course of study pursued preparatory to teaching, and whether he or she pursues the business of teaching as a permanent or a temporary employment.

The whole number of pupils, including classical and all others, belonging to the academy at the date of the report.

The whole number of pupils that have been taught during the whole or any part of the academic year for which the report is made.

The number of students belonging to the academy at the date of its report, or who belonged to it during part of the year, ending on the date of its report, and who are claimed by the trustees to have pursued for four months of said year or upwards, classical studies, or the higher branches of English education, or both, according to the true intent and meaning of this ordinance; said return also to designate how many of said scholars claimed are males, and how many females.

§ 5. The said report shall also contain, or have appended or annexed to it, a true catalogue or list of all the students belonging to the academy at the date of its report, or during part of the year ending on the date of its report, who are claimed by its trustees to be such classical scholars, or such scholars in the higher branches of English education or both, and to have pursued their studies for such length of time as to entitle them (or the academy to which they belong,) to a distributive share of the income of the Literature Fund, according to the true intent and meaning of this ordinance; in which said catalogue or list shall be inserted the name and age of each student claimed to be such scholar as aforesaid, together with a specification of the different studies pursued by such student, and the length of time the same were pursued in each quarter or term of the year ending on the date of said report, by recitations of ordinary frequency and in the ordinary way, designating said studies by the ordinary name or title of the book or treatise on the subject so studied, and designating also the part or portion of the book or treatise so studied; and the said catalogue or list shall also contain a declaration or certificate that all the students therein named, and claimed to be scholars as above described, had been found, on due examination, to have pursued all the studies, and acquired all the knowledge, required by this ordinance, as preliminary requisites to their becoming such scholars; and that this ordinance, in respect to exercises in composition and declamation, and in spelling, reading and writing, had been complied with.

§ 6. No students, in any such academy, shall be considered classical scholars within the meaning of this ordinance, until they shall have studied in such academy, or elsewhere, so much of the common elementary prose authors, in Latin, as is equal to one-half of the *Latin Reader, one-third of Cornelius Nepos, and two books of Cæsar's Commentaries, and in addition thereto, shall have read the first book of the Æneid of Virgil.*

§ 7. No such classical students shall entitle the institution to which they belong, to any share of the income of said fund unless it shall appear from the annual report of such institution, that they have pursued therein, for the space of four months or upwards of the year ending on the date of such report, the studies herein before declared to be preliminary to Virgil, together with the first book of the Æneid of Virgil, or other studies in the classics (either in Latin or Greek) usually pursued subsequent to the first book of the said Æneid; or shall, for a part of said period, have so pursued the said studies, or some of them, (including the said first book of the Æneid, or some of the said studies subsequent thereto) and for the residue of said period, shall have pursued the higher branches of English education, after they shall have become scholars therein as herein defined. *It being at the same time understood and so stated in the affidavit required from the principal, that all students so claimed as classical, shall have, previouly to being so claimed, pursued all the preliminary studies in arithmetic, English grammar and geography, hereby required from students claimed as such in the higher branches of English education, as more fully appears in the next section.*

§ 8. No students, in any academy, shall be considered scholars in the higher branches of English education, within the meaning of this ordinance, until they shall, on examination, be found to have attained due proficiency in the arts of reading and writing, and to have acquired due knowledge of the elementary rules or operations of arithmetic, commonly called notation, addition, subtraction, multiplication and division, as well in their compound as in their simple forms, and as well in vulgar and decimal fractions as in whole numbers together with the parts of arithmetic commonly called reduction, practice, the single rule of three direct and simple interest, and until they shall also, on such examination, be found to have studied so much of English grammar as to be able to parse correctly any common prose sentence in the English language, and to render into good English the common examples of bad grammar given in Murray's or Bullions', or some other like grammatical exercises; and shall also have studied some book or treatise on geography equal in extent to the duodecimo edition of Morse's, Woodbridge's or Mitchell's geography.

§ 9. No such scholars in the higher branches of English education, shall entitle the institution to which they belong to any share of said fund, unless it shall appear from the annual report of said institution, that they, after becoming such scholars, shall have pursued therein said higher branches of education, or some of them, for the space of four months or upwards of the year ending on the date of such report.

§ 10. All students belonging to any academy, and claimed by it to be classical scholars, or scholars in the higher branches of English education, or both, shall be exercised at convenient and ordinary intervals, *in spelling, reading and writing, and in the higher branches, viz: composition and declamation in the English language, (except that females need not be exercised in declamation) and in the annual reports of academies, it shall be stated how often, on an average, such students are exercised in each of the above.*

§ 11. No students belonging to any academy, shall hereafter be considered classical scholars, or scholars in the higher branches of English education, or both, so as to entitle the academy to which they belong, to any share of the income of the Literature Fund on their account, unless such students be of *the age of* TWELVE *years or upwards, at the time of making out the report in which they are claimed to be such scholars.*

The ages of the students so claimed, shall be added up at the foot of each page of the schedule, and *the ages of the whole be added up at the end of the schedule.*

GENERAL DIRECTIONS AND PROVISIONS AS TO REPORTS.

§ 12. And be it further ordained, that all reports or applications to the Regents, with all statements made in pursuance of this ordinance, as well as all other communications purporting to proceed from any academy, or from its trustees, as a corporate body, shall be submitted to the trustees of such academy at some stated or special meeting, legally held, at which a legal quorum shall be present ; and the same shall not be considered as a valid act or proceeding of such academy, until it be approved and adopted as such at such meeting, and be so declared to be, in its concluding or some other convenient part thereof. And when the same shall be so approved and adopted, and so declared to be, it shall, in order to secure satisfactory evidence thereof, be verified by the oath or affirmation of the president or other trustee who shall preside at said meeting, to be taken before some person authorized by law to administer oaths ; the trustees by their presiding officer, distinctly affirming that a legal quorum of said board was present at the adoption of the report.

§ 13. The affidavit required from the presiding officer of the board of trustees, and to immediately follow the annual report, shall be in the following words :

A. B. being duly sworn, (or affirmed as the case may be,) deposeth and saith, that he is one of the trustees of academy, (whose annual report to the Regents of the University immediately precedes this affidavit) that he officiated as the presiding officer at the meeting of the trustees of said academy referred to in the concluding part of the said report, and that the schedule hereunto annexed of the names, ages and studies of the students claimed, as stated therein, was submitted to the trustees at said meeting, and is believed by them to be correct, that said report, in all its parts, is made in the form required by the latest instructions received from the Regents of the University, and that the statement of facts therein set forth, are in all respects true according to the best of his knowledge, information and belief.

Sworn before me. &c.

AS TO GRAMMAR SCHOOLS OF COLLEGES, etc.

§ 14. It being provided by act of the Legislature, that the Regents of the University may, in their discretion, admit to a participation in the distribution of the said public moneys, any incorporated school, or school founded and governed by any literary corporation other than theological or medical, in which the usual academic studies are pursued, and which shall have been in like manner subjected to their visitation, and would in all other respects, were it incorporated as an academy, be entitled to such distribution; it is therefore, further ordained and declared, that all incorporated schools, or schools founded by literary corporations, which shall claim the benefit of the provisions above referred to, be required, in their application for such benefit, to set forth and show the particular grounds on which their claim thereto is founded, together with a general statement of their condition as to accommodations for instruction, course of studies pursued, and funds possessed by them; and that they also be required to make and transmit, with every such application to the Regents the same report in respect to the names, ages and studies of the students claimed by them to be classical students or students in the higher branches of English education, or both, as academies subject to the visitation of the Regents are now, or shall hereafter be required to make, in relation to the same subject matters.

AS TO ACADEMIES INCORPORATED BY THE LEGISLATURE.

§ 15. And whereas the Legislature, by providing in their act above referred to,* that any academy may subject itself to the visitation of the Regents, and become entitled to participate in the distribution of the public money, on its showing to the satisfaction of the Regents, that it is possessed of suitable academic grounds, buildings, library, and apparatus of the value of $2,500, have thereby established a rule, or prescribed a condition, for the admission of academies to the enjoyment of the public bounty, different from that before established or prescribed by the Regents;

And whereas the conditions on which academies may be incorporated, so as to become entitled to distributive shares of the public money, ought in the judgment of the Regents to be the the same, whether the application for such incorporation be made to them or to the Legislature;

Be it therefore further ordained, that all ordinances heretofore adopted by the Regents, on the subject of the incorporation of academies, be so modified in respect to the kind and value of property required to be possessed by the applicants for such incoporation, as to conform in that respect to the requirements of the statute above referred to.

*See page 13.

III. FORM OF ANNUAL REPORTS OF ACADEMIES.

The following is drafted in conformity to the preceding laws and ordinances, and may be considered as a safe guide. The Secretary has subjoined, in the form of notes, a statement of the more common omissions and defects in the annual reports.

PRELIMINARY DIRECTIONS.

1. *The reports are required to be engrossed on foolscap paper, and in the form of a book, and not in the form of law papers. A margin should be left at the back, so that they can be bound without concealing the writing.*

2. *The sheets containing the report and schedule, must be annexed to each other. This is sworn to, both by the President of the Board of Trustees and by the Principal.*

3. *The schedule of the Principal should not precede the report of the Trustees.*

4. *The various heads should be numbered, and instead of omitting any, because the answer is none, or something similar, it should be entered, with that remark. The omissions of this description are very numerous, as will be seen by referring to any (printed) annual report of the Regents, the words "not stated" being very common.*

5. *The reports are required to be transmitted to the Secretary on or before the first day of February in each year. In former years, allowance was made for the accidents of the season. There is now little or no excuse for delay.*

To the Regents of the University of the State of New-York:

The Trustees of   Academy established at   in the county of   *Respectfully Report:* That the condition of their academy on the   day of   A. D.   [here state the day on which the quarter ended nearest to the first of January,] in respect to the several subject matters required to be reported on by them, was as follows:

ACADEMIC PROPERTY.

For a particular statement of their academic lot, building, library, and apparatus, and for a general statement of their other property, the trustees refer to their report (or application) to the Regents, bearing date on or about the   day of   &c.

The property described in the report or application above referred to, remains, in respect to quantity, value, incumbrances, and in all other respects, the same as at the date of that report, or application, [or if any change has taken place, by the purchase of new property, or by improving the old, or in consequence of decline in value, from decay or any other cause, or if the incumbrances on it have been increased or diminished, state the fact according as it is, under the following heads :]

1. *Ground for Academy Buildings.**

State its present value. $

2. *Academy Buildings.*

Their present condition—whether out of repair—and what will put them in proper repair—their present actual value. $

3. *Academy Library.*†

Continue the catalogue of books added (if any) since the date of the last report, with their original cost and present value, in the following form :

Title or name of books arranged according to catalogue, if any, in use.	Number of volumes.	Original cost.	Present value.
Amount at date of last report, ...		$	$
[Give the total of each column.]		$	$

Give a general description of the condition of the books in the library in respect to their being new or old, in good order or worn out, &c., and deduct the value of such as have been lost or destroyed.

4. *Philosophical Apparatus.*‡

Continue this inventory also from the date of last report; including under it, besides what is strictily or technically philosophical apparatus, all instruments used in, or illustrative of any of the arts and sciences.

* *Ground for Academy Buildings.*—A common error under this head, as well as many others, is to state "*same as last year,*" "*same as in the last report.*" Every report should be complete in itself.

† *Academy Library.*—The value of the library is not unfrequently omitted, and the number of volumes in it, not stated, leaving these for the "*summary statement.*" Again, the volumes added since the last report, are occasionally not specified by their titles. The number of the volumes is also observed, in some instances, to be materially less than at the date of the previous report, and without any explanation being given.

‡ *Philosophical apparatus* —The defects and omissions are similar to the last. The articles purchased are sometimes not specified.

Description or name of each article.	Original cost.	Present value.
At date of last report, ...	$	$
	$	$

State the totals, and give a general description of the condition of the apparatus in respect to its being new or old, in good order or worn out, &c. Deduct the value of what is lost, broken or injured.

If the academy possess any mineralogical or botanical specimens, anatomical preparations, or any thing else illustrative of science or art, and not included as part of the library or apparatus already described, a general description of them should here be given, so as to convey a general idea of their extent, variety, character, &c.

5. *Title to Property, Incumbrances, &c.*

The said property is free from all incumbrances, (if such be the case.) If there be any incumbrance on it, state the general amount.

6. *Other Academic Property.*

The property of the academy, other than the academy lot, buildings, library and apparatus above described, consists of, [here describe in the most general terms, such as the following :]

Bonds and mortgages considered good, ... $
A house and lot, at, &c., worth, ...
One hundred acres of wild land, in, &c., worth, ...

Total, ... $

7. *Debts.*

The debts contracted by the academy which remained unpaid on the said day &c., including all arrears of interest (if any) and all outstanding or unpaid accounts acknowledged as debts, amounted on that day to $ (The amount of *incumbrances* as stated above in sec. 5, should be included.)

8. *Summary Statements.**

The total value of all the academic property above described is as follows:

Present value of academy lot and buildings, ... $
Present value of library, consisting of   volumes, (be careful to fill the blank with the number of volumes,.).......................................
Present value of philosophical apparatus,.............

Total value,.............................. $
Deduct for debts, if any, ...

Balance, showing value over and above all debts,...... $
Add for other property, valued at,....................

Total value of the whole,...................... $

9. *Books and Apparatus, compared with Catalogues, &c.*

All the books and articles of apparatus possessed by the academy have, during the year ending on the date of this report, been by or under the direction of the trustees, carefully examined and compared with the original catalogues or inventories of the books and apparatus belonging to the academy. And on such examination and comparison, all the books and apparatus belonging to the academy, and which ought to be in its possession, were duly found to be in such possession, in good order and condition, [or if any books or articles of apparatus be lost, missing, or damaged beyond what might reasonably be expected from ordinary wear and tear in their necessary use, so state the fact, specifying the particular books and articles of apparatus so lost or damaged, and stating also the name of the librarian or other person through whose act, omission or neglect, such loss or damage shall have happened.]

10. *Annual Revenue.*

Amount received or receivable for tuition in said academy during the year ending on the said   day of   &c., $
Amount received or receivable for interest or income of academic property, accrued during said year,........
Amount received during said year from the Regents of the University, on their annual apportionment of the income of the Literature Fund, ...

Total annual revenue,..... .... $

* *Summary Statements.*—This is a most important part of the report, and its omission, until supplied, subjects an academy to a suspension of payment. It is intended as a repetition of the items previously enumerated.

The order is sometimes inverted. The value of the *philosophical apparatus* is placed before that of the library.

N. B. The items above described should include only what accrued during the particular year above referred to. Any thing received in that year, for arrears accrued in former years, should not be included, the object of the statement being to show the true amount of revenue accrued, (whether paid or unpaid) for the particular year to which it refers, in order to enable the Regents to compare annual revenue with annual expenditures.

11. *Annual Expenditures.*

Amount paid or payable by the academy, for salaries or compensation of teachers, for the year ending on the said day of &c., ...	$
Amount paid or payable for interest (if any) accrued during said year, on debts outstanding against the academy, ...	
Amount paid or payable for repairs of buildings or other property belonging to the academy, made during said year, ...	
Amount paid or payable for fuel, and for all other incidental expenses, incurred by the academy during said year, ...	
Total annual expenditure, ...	$

N. B. The items above described should include only what was paid or payable on liabilities incurred by the academy for the particular year mentioned in the statement. Any thing paid in that year, on account of liabilities contracted or incurred in former years, should not be included—the object of the statement being to show the true amount of expenditures or liabilities for expenditures incurred, (whether actually paid or not,) during the particular year to which it relates, in order to enable us to compare annual expenditures with annual revenue, to see if the academy be falling in debt, or otherwise.

If any of the items of income or expenditure for any particular year happen to be either greater or less than the average for common years, the case should be stated according to the fact.

12. *Money received from Literature Fund.*

The moneys received from the Literature Fund for the last year, as stated in the preceding part of this report, under the head of revenue, together with all balances (if any) of such moneys received in former years, and suffered to remain on hand unexpended, have been expended during the last year, or are accounted for as follows: [Here state the fact as it is, always remembering, before any expenditure be made, that all such moneys are required by law to be expended or applied in paying the salaries or compensation of teachers.*]

*See Revised Statutes, chap. XV., art. 1, title 1, sec. 27, (being the Act of April 22, 1834,) and also the provisions of the Act passed April 17, 1838.

13. *Money raised and granted for the purchase of Books and Apparatus.*

If none has been received since the date of the last annual report, it is sufficient to state this. But if any has been received, the account should be stated as follows:

Amount raised by the trustees, ... $
Amount received from the Regents,..................

Total, ... $

which has been expended as follows:

(Here state what books or apparatus, or both, have been purchased, or refer particularly to them as enumerated under previous heads.)

If an unexpended balance remains to be accounted for, the disposition of it should be here stated.

14. *Departments.*

The departments of instruction established and in practical operation in the academy, are [here describe the different departments, if there be more than one, by reference to the subjects of instruction in each, or to the sex of the scholars attending it; and in all cases state whether male and female scholars are in the same or in different departments.]

15. *Teachers.*

The whole number of teachers employed in said academy on the said day of &c., was , of which number intend to make teaching a permanent profession.

The names, ages, qualifications and compensation of said teachers are as follows: [Here state the name of each teacher—the department in which he teaches—his age—how long he has followed the business of teaching—a general statement of the course of study pursued preparatory to becoming a teacher in said academy—if the teacher be a graduate of any college, the statement of that fact alone will be sufficient—if not such a graduate, specify in general terms the subjects studied by him, or compare them with the sub-graduate course of study pursued in any of our common colleges, and state what part or proportion of such a course they would form—or if they are equal to or exceed that course, so state the fact, either in reference to the time such teacher was first employed in the academy, or to the time of making its report—and in all cases state whether such teacher *intends* or *professes* an intention, to make teaching a permanent profession, or only a temporary occupation—state also the annual salary or compensation allowed to each teacher.]

16. *Subjects of study pursued, and class or text-book used.*

The subjects of study pursued in said academy, during said year, including classical and all others, with the class or text books used on each subject or study, were as follows:

[Here state all the subjects of study of every description, from the lowest to the highest, arranged in one column; and in the opposite column state the class or text-books used in studying it, as well in the lowest as in the highest departments; designating each book by its ordinary title and name of the author, thus:

Ordinary Elementary Studies.	*Text-books.*
Arithmetic,	Davies.
Book Keeping,	Preston.
Composition,	
Elocution,	
English Language, (Grammar,)	
do (Dictionary,)	
Geography,	
Orthography,	
Pronunciation, (standard,)	
Reading Books.	

Mathematics, &c.,

Algebra,
Astronomy, &c.

Languages,

Natural Sciences &c.,

Moral, Intellectual and Political Science,

In other words, the order adapted in schedule No. 9 of the annual report of the Regents, will be found to be at once the most convenient and satisfactory. The headings of "Ordinary Elementary Studies &c.," are not absolutely necessary, but the order should be preserved in conformity to the above divisions, otherwise academies are very apt to omit some of their most common studies, while others confound the subjects of study, placing for example "*Natural History*" under "*History.*" There is also frequently great uncertainty as to the reading books in use. Some give their common titles and omit the names of authors, while others only state the authors. It would be better to give both as, Murray's English Reader, Willson's American Class Reader.

17. *Spelling, Reading and Writing, and Composition and Declamation.*

The students required to be exercised in the above, were exercised therein, during said year, as often on an average as follows:
In Spelling, once a day (or once in days).
In Reading, once a day (or once in days).
In Writing, once a day (or once in days).
In Composition, once in days.
In Declamation (male students only), once in days, as appears by the affidavit of the Principal annexed to this report.

18. *Number of Students.*

A. The whole number of students (including classical and all others,) belonging to the academy on the said day of [Here insert the date given in the commencement of the report] was

B. The whole number of students (including classical and all others) that have been taught in the academy during the *year* ending on the said day of was

C. The number of students belonging to the academy on the said day of or who belonged to it during part of the year ending on that day, and who are claimed by the trustees to have pursued for four months of said year, or upwards, classical studies, or the higher branches of English education, or both, according to the true intent and meaning of the ordinance of the Regents of the 20th of October, 1853, was
Of whom all were males, (or all females,) or, of whom were males and were females.)

A schedule of the names, ages and studies of the said students, so claimed by the said trustees to have pursued classical studies, or the higher branches of English education, or both, is hereunto annexed, duly verified by oath, as required by the law of the State and the ordinance of the Regents.

19. *Prices or Rates of Tuition.*

The prices charged for tuition in said academy during said year were as follows: [Here state the different prices in reference to the different subjects taught, &c.]

20. *Gratuitous Instruction.*

If (as is known to be the case in some academies,) scholars be received from common schools, and gratuitously instructed, either as a reward of merit or otherwise, state under this head the number so received, with the grounds or principles *on which they are received, &c.* So if any scholars be received and instructed in the academy for services rendered by them, or on credit, to be paid for out of future earnings, &c., the fact *may* also be here stated.

21. *Academic Terms, Vacations, &c.*

The year is divided into terms, of weeks each, [or if they vary, mention the variation, with the length of each.]

There are weeks of vacation during the year, (enumerate these.)

22. *Price of Board.*

The average price of board in the vicinity of the academy, for scholars attending it from abroad, should be stated under this head, and if the principal or any of the teachers of the academy receive scholars into their private families, the terms may, if desired, be here stated.

23. *"Natural History of New-York."*

The "Natural History of New-York," in volumes, has been obtained for this academy, pursuant to provisions of law, from the Secretary of State. It continues up to the date of this report, to be the property of the academy, and is now in its library.*

(If *not* obtained, let that be stated.)

24. *Physical Education.*

(*Here state in particular whether any thing, and what is done as to ventilation and other subjects, referred to in the appendix, under "Physical Education."*)

25. *Conclusion and Authentication of Report.*

The preceding report from academy was submitted to the trustees of said academy, at a meeting legally held by them on the day of &c., at which meeting the following named trustees were present, (state names,) being a legal quorum of said Board of Trustees, and having been read and approved, it was duly adopted at said meeting as the report of said academy, and ordered (after being verified by the oath of the presiding officer at said meeting, and recorded on the minutes of its proceedings) to be transmitted to the Regents of the University, pursuant to the provisions of their ordinance in such case made and provided.

All which is hereby done in obedience to said order this day of &c.

A. B., *President, or President pro tem.*
(*As the case may be*)
of Academy.

* The Regents are under the necessity of requiring this report, since improper attempts have been made to take these volumes as the property of individual trustees or of principals.

AFFIDAVIT ABOVE REFERRED TO.

County of ss:

A. B., being duly sworn, (or affirmed as the case may be,) deposeth and saith, that he is one of the trustees of academy, (whose annual report to the Regents of the University immediately precedes this affidavit,) that he officiated as the presiding officer at the meeting of the trustees of said academy, referred to in the concluding part of said report; and that the schedule hereunto annexed of the names, ages and studies of the students claimed, as stated therein, was submitted to the trustees at said meeting, and is believed by them to be correct; that said report in all its parts, is made in the form required by the latest instructions received from the Regents of the University; and that the statement of facts therein set forth, is in all respects true according to the best of his knowledge, information and belief.

A. B.

Sworn before me this day of &c.

The Schedule of the Principal of the Academy makes up the residue of the Report in the following form :

The following is the statement (referred to in the annexed report from Academy,) of the names, ages and studies of the students claimed by the Trustees of the said academy to have pursued, for four months or upwards, of the year mentioned in said report, classical studies, or the higher branches of English education, or both, according to the true intent and meaning of the ordinance of the Regents of the 20th of October, 1853, with a specification of the different studies pursued by each of said students, and the length of time the same were pursued in each quarter or term of said year, said studies being designated by the ordinary name or title of the book or treatise studied, and the part or portion of each book so studied being also stated, with the time spent in studying the same, during each ef said terms.

No. and name of student.	Age.	Studies pursued for the quarter or term ending the	Studies pursued for the quarter or term ending the	Studies pursued for the quarter or term ending the	Studies pursued for the quarter or term ending the
1. A. B.	15	$\frac{1}{2}$ of Paley's Moral Philosophy, 3 m. 3 first books of Euclid, 2 m.	Paley's Moral Philosophy, fin. 3 m. 3 next books of Euclid, 3 m.	100 pages of Cicero de Oratore, 3 m. 2 books of Cæsar's Com. 2 m.	3 books of Virgil's Æneid, 3 m. 40 pages Græca Minora, 2 m.
2. C. D.	14	Same as No. 1.	Same as No. 1.	$\frac{1}{2}$ Blair's Lec. on Rhet, 3 m. Bonnycastle's Algebra, to Quadratic Equations, 3 m.	$\frac{1}{2}$ of Gibson's Surveying, 3 m. $\frac{1}{2}$ of Tytler's History, 2 m.
3. E. F.	16	Latin Grammar, 3 m. $\frac{1}{2}$ of Corderius, 2 m.	$\frac{1}{4}$ of Viri Romæ, 3 m. $\frac{1}{4}$ of Jacob's Latin Reader, 2 m.	3 books Caesar's Com. 3 m. Greek Grammar, 2 m.	2 books of Cæsar's Com. 1 m. 2 books of the Æneid, 2 m. 10 pages of Græca Minora, 1 m.
4. G. H.	13	Same as No. 3.	Same as No. 3.	Same as No. 3.	2 books of Cæsar's Com. 1 m. 2 books of Virgil's Æneid, 2 m. $\frac{1}{4}$ of Tytler's History, 2 m.
Total ages.	58				

The ages to be added at the foot of each page, and the total ages may also be given.

At the close of the schedule, an affidavit should be added in the following form:

County of *ss.*—A. B. being duly sworn, deposeth and saith, that he is principal instructor of academy, whose annual report to the Regents of the University is hereunto annexed; that the said report is made in conformity to the latest instructions received from the Regents of the University: that the annexed (or preceding) schedule contains a true statement of the names, ages and studies of the several students belonging to said academy on the day of , or who belonged to it during part of the year ending on that day, and who are claimed to have pursued, for four months of said year or upwards, classical studies, or the higher branches of English education, or both, acording to the true intent and meaning of the ordinance of the Regents of the 20th of Oct., 1853, that none *of the said students are under the age of* TWELVE *years, and that such of them as are claimed to be classical students have actually pursued all the prèliminary studies (both Latin and English) required by the 6th and 7th sections of said ordinance, to make them such students* and have also read the first book of the Æneid of Virgil; that such of them as are claimed to be students in the higher branches of English Education, had *before they were considered as such students,* attained such proficiency in reading and writing, and acquired such elementary or preliminary knowledge as is required by the 8th section of said ordinance, that they have all subsequently pursued the requisite studies and performed the requisite exercises in composition and declamation, and in *spelling, reading and writing,* and for the period of time required by said ordinance to entitle said academy to a distributive share of the income of the Literature Fund; the said exercises in composition and declamation having been as often, on an *average,* as once in days: *in spelling, once in days; in reading, once in days; and in writing, once in days.* All which this deponent affirms to be true, according to the best of his knowledge, information and belief.

A. B. *Principal &c.*

Sworn, &c.

In cases of the death or absence of the principal, the schedule should be made and sworn to by some other teacher, if there be any acquainted with the facts to be stated; or if there be no such other teacher, it must be made and sworn to by some one of the trustees, stating the reason of his making it, the sources of his knowledge or information, with his belief as to its correctness, &c.

NOTES.

As the amount of moneys appropriated to each academy depends on the number of students allowed by the Regents, it is extremely important that the schedule of the Principal should be correct in all its parts. The most common defects and omissions are as follows:

A. An endeavor to crowd the enumeration for three and even four terms on a single page of foolscap. This leads to contraction of the names of text-books—t indistinctness and uncertainty as to the quantity studied, and if, (as is frequently the case,) no lines be drawn so as to separate the name and studies of one student from another, to confusion in designating what belongs to each.

B. In one or two instances the principal has returned all his scholars, whether claimed or not, in his schedule, and then annexed marks to distinguish the former. I am directed to say, that in future *all similar schedules will be returned for correction.*

C. The *names* of students claimed are sometimes omitted, and the number stands a blank.

D. More commonly there is a blank in the column of *age*. It has been an invariable rule of the Regents of the University for many years *to reject all students whose ages are not given. "Where age is omitted it will be presumed to be less than twelve years."*

E. It occasionally happens that separate returns are made of each term or quarter, and the studies pursued in it, and thus the name of the student claimed has to be followed over various parts of the schedule. This also will be returned for correction.

F. *Insufficient Studies.*

I reprint the following remarks contained in previous editions of these instructions:

In respect to classical studies, the statute provides that no student shall be deemed to have pursued classical studies, unless he shall have advanced at least so far as to have read in Latin the first book of the Æneid. What particular studies are to make up the intermediate stage of the advance, or what in other words shall precede Virgil, not being specified in the statute, it became necessary for the Regents to specify it, which they accordingly did by their ordinance of 1828, *and now again by their ordinance of October 20th,* 1853. The quantum of Latin study required to precede Virgil being thus expressly defined, in terms of the plainest possible import, it was not expected to be misapprehended or overlooked. Yet it has heretofore often been, and sometimes still is, a subject of the most unaccountable misapprehension or neglect. Students passing directly from grammar, or other like elementary studies, into Virgil, in almost total disregard of the intermediate course prescribed by the Regents, are not only claimed to be classical scholars under the ordinance above referred to, but are sworn to be such by the affidavit of the teacher, which is thus falsified by his own showing.

Both the statute of the State, and the ordinance of the Regents above referred to, provide that no one shall be considered a classical student, until he shall have completed a prescribed course of study, ending with the first book of the Æneid ; and as it is provided in another part of the statute, that classical studies shall be pursued for four months in each year, to entitle a student to a share of the public money, it might at first view be inferred that the four months here required must elapse *after* a student becomes *such* a classical one, that is, after his having completed the prescribed course above referred to. But such an inference is not in accordance with the construction given by the Regents to the law, which only provides *when* a student shall be considered classical for certain specified purposes. It does not define or alter classical studies. So that if the prescribed course ending with the first book of the Æneid be completed, and four months be spent in doing it, the requirements of the statute are satisfied, as much as if the four months had been spent in studies subsequent to Virgil.

In respect to English studies, the statute provides that no student shall be deemed to have pursued the higher branches of English education, unless he shall have advanced beyond such knowledge of Arithmetic, English Grammar and Geography, as is usually obtained in common schools. The studies preliminary to the higher branches of English education, which are here stated only in general terms, are more particularly prescribed and defined in the ordinance of the Regents above referred to; but neither that ordinance, nor the statute on which it is founded, prescribes or defines what shall constitute the higher branches of such education. And hence it often occurs in academic reports, that certain studies are claimed to have the rank of higher branches of education, which are not allowed by the Regents to be of that character. The following extract from a report made by a committee of the Regents in 1829, will exhibit the views *then* entertained on this subject, which have not been *since* materially varied:

"The ordinance of the Regents, prescribing the requisites and forms of the academic reports, defines the studies which shall be considered preliminary to the higher branches of English education, but does not define what those higher branches shall be. This omission in the ordinance is understood to have been made, partly on account of the difficulty of embracing in any definition, all the subjects of study which deserve the rank of higher branches of education; but chiefly for the purpose of reserving to the Regents the right of determining what shall be considered the higher branches of education, as they shall from time to time, be presented in the academic reports. In the exercise of this reserved right, the committee have had no difficulty in considering all kinds of History, Geometry, Algebra, Botany, Rhetoric, Natural and Moral Philosophy, Logic, Chemistry, Book-Keeping, Surveying, Mensuration, Navigation, Astronomy, Trigonometry, Constitution of the United States, or of this State, Grecian and Roman Antiquities, higher parts of Arithmetic, if particularly specified, Geography, with the use of Globes or Mapping, as entitled to be ranked among the higher branches of education; but they have had some difficulty in determining on the character which ought to be given to the study of modern languages other than English, such as French, German, Spanish, &c. These subjects of study do not strictly come within the range of an English education, nor can they be considered parts of the classics. They nevertheless appear to the committee to be equivalent in merit to most other subjects of study which are specially favored by the Regents. The committee have, therefore, placed the students engaged in these studies on a par with classical scholars, or scholars in the higher branches of English education.

"In some of the academic reports, Geography, English Grammar and Arithmetic, are claimed to be higher branches of English education; but in all cases where such a claim has been made without any specification to show what particular parts of those branches have been studied, the committee have invariably rejected the claim, considering such studies not above the ordinary grade of studies in common schools."

Another committee of the Regents, in a subsequent report on the same subject, made with special reference to the study of Geography, submitted the following remarks:

"In the report of the committee of distribution for the last year, the study of Geography, with the use of the Globes or Mapping, was included among the studies appertaining to the higher branches of English education. The present committee do not propose to reverse the decision of their predecessors in respect to that study, but only to add what they consider an implied qualification of it. Geography, with the use of Globes, is rightly considered as one of the higher branches of English education, provided the study of it be pursued at a proper time and in a proper way. The proper time for such a study is after the student has gone through with the elementary books on Geography; and the proper mode of studying the use of the Globes is by demonstrating or performing the problems relating to the Globe, as laid down in any of the approved works on the subject. The study of Geography in its elementary stages, accompanied by an exhibition of the Globes, or a reference to the use of them, or by the exercise of Mapping, is not such a study as was intended to come within the definition of any of the higher branches of any English education."

In a still later report on the same or similar subjects, the following remarks were submitted:

"In some reports, Geography, with the use of Globes, is claimed to be among the higher branches of English education, without any designation of the kind of Geography studied, &c., but such claim cannot be allowed; none of the elementary books on Geography can be considered '*higher branches of education,*' they are expressly declared by the act of the Legislature and the ordinance of the Regents, as before referred to, to be preliminary to the higher branches. But after the elementary study of Geography be completed, if the student enter on the study of the more advanced parts of it, such as Physical Geography, &c., as found in the largest edition of Woodbridge, Malte-Brun, &c., and especially if such study be accompanied by exercises on the Globes, it ought to be considered among the higher branches of education, and where its character is shown by sufficient specification in the reports, it has been uniformly so considered by the Regents. The same remark may be made in respect to Arithmetic; its elementary parts, as defined in the ordinance of 1828, not being considered among the higher branches, but the more advanced parts, if sufficiently specified, being so considered.

"What actually constitutes the higher branches of English education, is not defined by any act of the Legislature, nor by any ordinance of the Regents. This omission is not accidental, but is owing to causes which have been fully stated in former reports made by committees of distribution, and published for the information of the academies. But the studies required to precede the higher branches of education are specially defined in both the law of the State and the ordinance of the Regents; and it was certainly reasonable to expect that none of the studies thus declared to be preliminary to the higher branches, would be put forth as part of such branches; but such expectations have not been realised. In some of the reports, such studies, or others equally inferior, have been treated as higher branches of education, but the claim to have them so considered has, in all cases, been overruled by the committee."

It will be observed, on attentively perusing the ordinance of the Regents of the 18th of March, 1828, that there is a material difference between classical students and students in the higher branches of English education, in respect to the mode of computing the period of study. If a student spend four months of the year in classical studies preliminary to Virgil, and in the first book of the Æneid of Virgil, he is a classical student, within the meaning of the ordinance under consideration;* but if he spend any length of time in the studies preliminary to the higher branches of English education, [specified in the second section of the said ordinance,] he does not thereby entitle the institution to which he belongs to any share of the public money; he must, *after* having actually pursued all the preliminary studies, and acquired all the knowledge prescribed in the second section of said ordinance, have spent at least four months of the year in the study of the higher branches of English education. If the distinction here stated, between classical and other studies, be well understood, much of the difficulty heretofore experienced in making out the academic reports will be obviated.

G. *Insufficient Description of Studies.*

The statute so often above referred to requires a description or particular statement of the studies pursued by each pupil, with the books studied in whole or in part; and if in part, what part.

The subjects of study, as well as the books used in studying them, are here required to be stated. It is not sufficient to state either alone. In some instances, the subject studied, such as History, Astronomy, &c., is stated without any mention of the text-books used; but as the extent and character of any study depend much on the books used, such a description must be considered entirely insufficient.

Another instance of insufficient description, is where studies are described by the words *the same as last;* leaving it uncertain whether the last preceding

* The comment here made, being taken from the former editions of these Instructions, had reference to the ordinance of 1828. *By the ordinance of October 20, 1853, (see sec. 7) a student cannot be reported as a classical scholar, until he has gone through with the same preliminary course of study as is required of the students in the higher branches of English education.*

term or last preceding student be referred to. Such references are proper when there is no ambiguity attending them, as in the form herewith published.

But the common fault, under the head of insufficient description lies in not stating how much of each book is studied. In such cases we are to intend that the whole book has been read, yet as the time spent on it is given, it often falsifies such intendment, as well as the affidavit of the teacher, in which such intendment is in *effect* sworn to. To specify all such particulars is, I am aware, attended with a great deal of labor, and not unfrequently with great difficulty, particularly where there are changes of teachers during the year for which the report is made. But as both the law of the State, and the ordinance of the Regents, require the trustees or their teachers to state the part of each book studied during each term, with the time spent on it, &c., the duty cannot be dispensed with.

If there be only three terms in any academy during the year, that is, if any term be intended to be one-third of a year, although on account of vacations, it may not embrace four full months, yet for all practical purposes it may be considered as four months.

H. *Term of Study in each Academic year.*

In some few academies, scholars who have not pursued classical studies, or the higher branches of English education four months of the year, ending on the date of the annual report, but who, having pursued such studies for four months, including fractional parts of the previous year, not covered by the report of that year, are reported and claimed to have pursued the requisite studies, for the requisite time, to entitle the institution to which they belong, to a distributive share of the public money on their account; thus adding together fractions of time in two different academic years, to make up the whole period of four months required for a single year. But all such claims have been invariably rejected; the law of the State and the ordinance of the Regents requiring in the most explicit terms, the time of study to be four months of the *year* ending on the date of the report. The Regents allow the trustees of each academy to arrange the terms or sessions of their academic year, as they think proper; but they are required to make their report for the year ending with the close of the term nearest to the first of January; and when the terms are so established. the academic year must be governed by them. Fractions of time in one year, can in no case be used for another year.

IV. Distribution of moneys granted to Academies, and forms necessary to obtain the amount allotted to each Academy.

The Literature Fund is now under the care and management of the Comptroller of the State, in the same manner as the Common School Fund. The apportionment or distribution of its income among academies, is made by the Regents of the University, annually, on or before the 1st of March. As soon as the apportionment is made, *it is published in the State paper for the time being*, and certfied by the Chancellor and Secretary of the University to the Comptroller, on whose warrant the amount apportioned to each academy will be paid by the Treasurer of the State, on drafts or orders therefor drawn on him by the treasurers of the several academies; such drafts or orders being accompanied by a proper certificate from the president or secretary of the academy, under its corporate seal, that the person signing the draft is the treasurer of the academy, duly appointed by the trustees thereof. The draft may be in the following form:

To the Treasurer of the State of New-York:

Pay to or order, the amount of money apportioned or to be apportioned during the present year, to Academy, by the Regents of the University, out of the income of the Literature Fund.

Dated, &c. A. B. *Treasurer of Academy.*

STATE OF NEW-YORK, } ss.
County of }

It is hereby certified, that A. B., the person signing the above draft or order, is the treasurer of Academy, above named, duly appointed by the Trustees thereof; and that the said draft was duly signed by him.

In witness whereof, the corporate seal of said adcademy is hereon impressed, this day of, &c.

[L. S.] C. D., *President or Secretary* (as the case may be) *of Academy.*

If there be no seal of the academy, that fact should be stated in the certificate.

N. B. A similar form must be used in all cases where money is to be drawn from the Comptroller.

V. Applications for money to purchase books and apparatus.

I. LAW OF THE STATE.

[See Title 1, Article 1, Section 20.]

[This is the act, passed April 22, 1834.]

[This law is continued under the provisions of the present constitution, by annual or biennial enactment. The amount granted however, varies in different years.]

II. ORDINANCE OF THE REGENTS.

Passed October 20, 1853.

Being a consolidation of all the ordinances, resolutions and decisions of the Regents on the subject, as contained in the "Instructions" printed in 1849.

The Regents of the University having been empowered, by an act of the Legislature "*relating to the distribution and application of the revenues of the Literature Fuud,*" passed April 23, 1834, and also by several successive acts passed from time to time, in conformity thereto, to assign in their discretion, to the several academies and schools subject to their visitation, certain portions of said revenue, not exceeding $250, a year to any one of said academies and schools, to be applied to the purchase of text-books, maps and globes, or philosophical or chemical apparatus for the use of the same, subject to such rules and regulations as the said Regents may prescribe, and the said act of April 1834, containing also the following proviso, and which by successive enactments, is continued to the present time. "But no part of said excess, (i. e, of the money granted) shall be actually paid over, unless the Trustees of the academy or school to which it is to be appropriated, shall raise or apply an equal sum of money to the same object."

The Regents do therefore ordain and declare,

1. That no part of the revenue of the Literature Fund, to be assigned to any academy or school for the purpose contemplated by the above recited provision of law, shall be paid over to such academy or school, until the Trustees thereof shall certify and declare under their corporate seal, that the money required as above to be raised and applied by them for the said purposes, has been raised by contribution, donation, or from other sources independent of their own corporate property, that the said money has been so raised or contributed with the express view of applying for and receiving a like sum from the Regents for the purpose contemplated in said act, and that the same has been actually paid to their treasurer to be applied for the purpose above mentioned, designating such purposes by specifying the particular books, maps and articles of apparatus proposed to be purchased by them, and classifying them as taken from the list or catalogue of the Regents or not.

2. That whenever (but not oftener than once a year) the Trustees of any such academy or school, shall present to the Regents, the certificate required by the preceding section, and the matters contained therein be satisfactory to them, they, the said Regents, will appropriate a sum of money equal to what shall appear from said certificate to have been raised for the purpose therein specified, not however to exceed the sum of two hundred and fifty dollars.

3. The money so raised and granted shall be applied in the purchases specified in such certificate, but the Regents reserve the right to disapprove of a part or the whole of said proposed purchases, and to designate and direct what may be purchased in lieu thereof or of part thereof, notice of the articles so to be designated and substituted to be given to said Trustees.

4. Whenever any appropriation shall thus be made by the Regents it shall be the duty of the Chancellor and Secretary of the University to certify the same to the Comptroller of the State, that the same may be paid by him according to the statute in such case made and provided.

5. The statute of April 1834, and the several laws passed in conformity thereto, do not apply to the sums of money required for the endowment of an academy, viz. $150 for the purchase of a library and $150 for the purchase of an apparatus.

6. Contributions of books, minerals &c., shall not be considered as a sufficient compliance with the above requirements; but the contributions shall be in actual money.

7. The term "text-book," contained in the above recited act, is construed to include all standard books, whether designed for use as class or text-books or otherwise.

8. Every academy to whom moneys shall be granted, for the purchase of books and apparatus, is hereby required to report to the Regents, in its next annual report, presented after said grant, the full and complete expenditure of all moneys, both raised and granted, for the above purpose, and until it does so account, the Regents will withhold the amount unaccounted for, from the respective share of each academy, in the distribution of the revenue of the Literature and United States Deposit funds. Nor will the Regents make any new appropriation to such academy, unless the above requisition has been fully complied with.

9. Whenever there shall be applications to this Board for appropriations of money to purchase books and apparatus, and there shall not be a sufficient amount on hand to grant all such applications, the preference shall be given to those academies which shall, at the time, have received the least amount from the Literature Fund for that purpose.

10. Whenever applications shall come before the Board at its first annual meeting, or any subsequent adjourned meeting, before the annual report of the Board to the Legislature shall be adopted* from academies which shall have received appropriations of money

*This is always a *very few* days preceding the 1st of March in each year.

for the purchase of books and apparatus, such applications shall be reserved until that time, for the purpose of ascertaining whether other applications shall be made from academies not having received such appropriations.

III. FORM OF AN APPLICATION FOR MONEY TO PURCHASE BOOKS AND APPARATUS.

To the Regents of the University of the State of New-York :

"The trustees of Academy respectfully represent that they have raised, or caused to be raised, the sum of dollars, to be applied to the purchase of books and apparatus, pursuant to the act of the Legislature relating to the distribution and application of the revenues of the Literature Fund, passed April 22, 1834; that the said sum has been raised by donations or contributions from *sources independent of their own corporate property :* that the *same has been actually paid to their treasurer ; that the said money has been so raised or contributed with the express view* of applying for and receiving a like sum from the Regents for the purpose contemplated in said act, and that it is intended to apply the said sum of money, together with the money hereby applied for pursuant to said act, to the purchase of the books and articles of apparatus particularly specified in the schedule hereunto annexed.

The said trustees therefore hereby apply to the Regents of the University for an appropriation to the said academy of the sum of dollars out of the moneys mentioned in the said act, to be applied, together with the like sum raised by them as above mentioned, to the purposes stated in said schedule, pursuant to the provisions of the act above referred to.

Done by the trustees of said academy at a legal meeting held the day of &c., at which meeting the following named trustees were present, [state names,] and having been read and approved, it was duly adopted at the said meeting as the application of said academy, and ordered (after being verified by the oath of the presiding officer at said meeting and recorded on the minutes of its proceedings) to be transmitted to the Regents of the University pursuant to the provisions of their ordinance in such case made and provided.

All which is hereby done in obedience to said order this day of &c.

A. B., *President, or President pro tem.*
(As the case may be)
of Academy.

This application must be verified by the oath of the president or person presiding at the meeting of the trustees, when it was directed to be made.

The Schedule

Of books and apparatus proposed to be purchased must then be annexed. And in preparing it, classify the *books* proposed to be purchased, thus:

1. Books selected from the list prepared by the Regents.
2. Books not taken from the Regents' list.

   Then

3. Apparatus.*

IV. A FORM OF A DRAFT FOR MONEY APPROPRIATED TO AN ACADEMY FOR THE PURCHASE OF BOOKS AND APPARATUS.

To the Treasurer of the State of New-York:

Pay to or order, the sum of dollars appropriated by the Regents of the University on the day of 185 to Academy for the purchase of books and apparatus.

Dated, &c. A. B. *Treasurer of Academy.*

(This draft must be accompanied by a certificate in the form given on page 83.)

[The Regents have decided that Zoological, Botanical and Mineralogical specimens cannot be purchased under the provisions of the laws and ordinances at the commencement of this section.] (Minutes, February 20, 1845.)†

5. *Recommendation of books and apparatus to be purchased by academies.*

Several academies having, in their applications for money to purchase books and apparatus, requested the Regents to designate the particular books and articles of apparatus most suitable for them to purchase, it was referred by the Regents to their standing committee on the appropriation of money for the purchase of books and apparatus to make, in all such caees, the designation requested.

The committee above referred to, prepared, in pursuance of the above order of reference, Feb. 5, 1839, a list of books recommended by them, which is here published for the information of academies.

Books.

The following list is furnished for the purpose of indicating the kinds of books which the Regents of the University consider proper to constitute libraries for the academies; but it is not intended to restrict the academies exclusively to this list in making their selections. If other books are desired, the propriety of allowing them to be purchased will be determined by the board when applications for the appropriation of money for the purpose shall be made. In the catalogues accompanying all such applications, the selection from the following lists will be distinguished from selections not made from it, by placing them in different columns, with these captions, viz:

*These applications should not be sent, inclosed in or annexed to the annual report, but seperate and properly endorsed. The moneys are never granted until on or after the 1st of March, and the applications must therefore be received by at least the middle of February.

† The Regents have also decided that musical instruments cannot be so purchased.

1. Books selected from the list prepared by the Regents.
3. Books not taken from the Regents' list.*

THEOLOGY AND ECCLESIASTICAL HISTORY.

Chalmers' Evidences and Authority of Christian Revelation.
Butler's Analogy.
Burnet's History of the Reformation.
Hannah Adams' View of all Religions.
Josephus' Works.
Watson's Apology.
Paley's Evidences of Christianity.
Pilgrim's Progress.
Wollaston's Religion of Nature.
Buck's Theological Dictionary.
Paley's Natural Theology.
McIlvine's Evidences of Christianity.
Prideaux's Connections.

HISTORY, BIOGRAPHY AND ANTIQUITIES.

Bancroft's History of the United States.
Ramsay's History of the United States.
Grahame's History of the United States.
Botta's History of the American Revolution.
Hume's History of England with Smollett and Bissett's Continuation.
Goldsmith's History of England.
Mackintosh's History of the Revolution of 1688.
Russell's History of Ancient and Modern Europe.
Gibbon's Roman Empire.
Ferguson's Roman Republic.
Goldsmith's History of Rome.
Niebuhr's History of Rome.
Sparks' American Biography.
Tytler's Universal History.
Robertson's Historical Works.
Millot's Ancient and Modern History.
Hallam's History of the Middle Ages.
Belknap's History of New-Hampshire.
Hutchinson's History of Massachusetts.
Smith's History of New-York.
Eastman's History of New-York.
Smith's History of New-Jersey.
Trumbull's History of Connecticut.
O'Callaghan's History of New-Netherlands.
Williamson's History of North Carolina.
Williams' History of Vermont.
Bozman's History of Maryland.
Watson's Life of Philip II.
Watson's Life of Philip III.
De Stael on the French Revolution.
Heeren's Historical Works.
Bolingbroke's Letters on History.
Botta's Italy under Napoleon.
Gordon's History of Ireland.
Molina's History of Chili.
Southey's History of Brazil.
Mills' History of Chivalry.
Mills' History of the Crusaders.
Murphy's Tacitus.
Thompson's Suetonius.
Hampton's Polybius.
Athens, its Rise and Fall, by Bulwer.
Wheaton's History of the Northmen.
Lee's Memoirs of the War in the Southern States.
Schiller's Thirty Years' War in Germany.
Kennet's Roman Antiquities.
Adam's Roman Antiquities.
Potter's Grecian Antiquities.

* For various reasons, it has not been deemed advisable to enlarge this catalogue by a selection from works published subsequently to the date of this report. A few books have been added, on the request of authors, and on the recommendation of committees of the Regents.

Archæologia Americana.
Marshall s Life of Washington.
Sparks' Life of Washington.
Ramsay's Life of Washington.
Life of Lafayette.
Franklin s Life and Essays.
Irving's Life of Columbus.
Middleton's Life of Cicero.
Wirt's Life of Patrick Henry.
Voltaire's Life of Peter the Great.
Voltaire's Life of Charles the XII.
Plutarch's Lives.
Prescott's Historical Works.
Cooper's History of the Navy.
Boswell's Life of Johnson.
Biography of the Signers of the Declaration of Independence.
Lempriere's Universal Biography.
Elliot s American Biographical Dictionary.
Labaume's Campaign of Napoleon in Russia.
Sully's Memoirs.
Gould's Abridgement of Alison's History of Europe.
Sears' Pictorial History of the United States.
Squires' Indian Antiquities.

JURISPRUDENCE, POLITICS AND COMMERCE.

Secret Debates in the Convention of the United States.
Beck's Medical Jurisprudence.
Blackstone's Commentaries.
Kent's Commentaries.
Federalist.
Debates in the New-York Convention.
Diplomacy of the United States.
Miller's View of the English Government.
Everett's Europe.
Everett's America.
Ferguson's Civil Society.
Junius, (Woodfall's)
Malthus on Population.
Malthus on Political Economy.
Debates in the Massachusetts Convention.
Debates in the Virginia Convention.
Montesquieu s Spirit of Laws.
Aristotle s Ethics and Politics, [Gillies' Translation.]
Puffendorf's Law of Nature and Nations.
Ricardo s Political Economy.
Say's Political Economy.
Vethake s Political Economy.
Wayland s Political Economy.
McVickar's Political Economy.
Vattell s Law of Nations.
Grotius.
Washington's Letters.
Lord Brougham's Speeches.
Adam Smith's Wealth of Nations, [McCulloch's Edition.]
Bentham on Morals and Legislation.
Constitutions of the States.
Miss Martineau s Illustrations of Political Economy.
The Madison Papers.
De Tocqueville.

PERIODICAL AND COLLECTIVE WORKS.

Silliman's Journal.
Encyclopœdia Americana.
Nicholson's Encyclopœdia.
Treasury of Knowledge.
Annals of Education.
The Cultivator.
Harper's Classical Series.
Harper's Family Library.
Lardner's Cabinet Cyclopædia.

Library of Entertaining Knowledge.
The Penny Cyclopædia.
The Penny Magazine.
The Library of Useful Knowledge.
T. Dwight's American Magazine.

ARTS AND SCIENCES.

INCLUDING NATURAL PHILOSOPHY, NATURAL HISTORY,

Brande's Dissertation on Chemical Philosophy.
Emerson's Mechanics.
Ferguson's Astronomy.
Goods' Book of Nature.
Haine's on the New-York Canals.
Keith on the Globes.
Nicholson's Natural Philosophy.
Playfair's History of Natural Philosophy.
Rumford's Essays.
Chemistry applied to Agriculture.
Bakewell's Introduction to Geology.
How to observe Geology.
De la Beche's Geological Manual.
Cuvier's Animal Kingdom.
Arnott's Physics.
Bridgewater Treatises.
Cleveland's Mineralogy.
Bigelow's Technology.
Lyell's Geology.
Phillip's Guide to Geology.
Peale's Graphics.
Yale College Mathematics.
Cambridge Mathematics.
Hutton's Mathematics.
Bourdon's Algebra, by Davies.
Davies' Mathematical Works.
Gibson's Surveying.
Gummere's Surveying.
Olmsted's Philosophy.
Cambridge Course of Philosophy.
Websters' Manual of Chemistry.
Parkes' Chemical Catechism.
Beck's Chemistry.
Burritt's Geography of the Heavens.
Wallace on the Globes.
Wayland's Moral Philosophy.
Upham's Intellectual Philosophy.
Scientific Class Book.
Enfield's Philosophy.
Comstock's Mineralogy.
" Botany.
" Chemistry.
" Natural Philosophy.
Smellie's Philosophy of Natural History.
Cuvier's Revolutions of the Globe.
" Theory of the Earth.
Shepard's Mineralogy.
Cousin's History of Philosophy.
Laplace's Mechanique Celeste, (Translated by Bowditch.)
Newton's Principia.
Nuttall's Ornithology.
Wilson's Ornithology.
Bowditch's Navigation.
Whateley's Logic and Rhetoric.
Ure's Chemical and Mineralogical Dictionary.
Sir Humphrey Davy's Elements of the Philosophy of Chemistry.
Rush on the Human Voice.
Beck's Botany.
Dana's Mineralogy.
Sganzin's Civil Engineering.
Hassler's Mathematical Tables.
Farrar's Electricity and Magnetism.
Godman's Natural History.

VOYAGES AND TRAVELS, GEOGRAPHICAL AND STATISTICAL WORKS.

Bruce's Travels in Abyssinia.
Park's Travels in Africa.
Lewis and Clarke's Travels to the Pacific Ocean.
Pitkin's Statistical View of the United States.
Long's Expedition to the Rocky Mountains.
Parry's First, Second and Third Voyages.
Shaler's Sketch of Algiers.
Anson's Voyage round the World.
Boswell's Tour to the Hebrides.
Chateaubriand's Travels in Greece and Egypt.
Clarke's Travels in Russia.
" Travels in Greece, Egypt and Holy Land.
Cook's Voyages.
Belzoni's Travels in Egypt.
Eustace's Classical Tour through Italy.
Forsyth's Italy.
John Bell's Italy.
Franklin's Journey to the Polar Sea.
Russel's Tour in Germany.
Heber's Travels in India.
Humboldt's Personal Narrative of his Travels in South America.
Jefferson's Notes on Virginia.
Johnson's Journey to the Hebrides.
Malcolm's Sketches of Persia.
Mavor's Collection of Voyages and Travels.
Poinsett's Notes on Mexico.
Schoolcraft's Travels.
Silliman's Travels in England, Scotland and Holland.
Carter's Letters from Europe.
Hobhouse's Albania.
Lamartine's Pilgrimage.
Laborde's Petræa.
Captain Back's Expedition.
Stephens' Travels.
Amherst's Embassy to China.
A Year in Spain.
Barrow's Visit to Iceland.
Dwight's Travels in Germany.
Woodbridge and Willard's Ancient and Modern Geography.
Malte-Brun's Geography.
Balbi's Geography.
Brooks and Marshall's Universal Gazetteer.
Simond's Switzerland.
Gordon's Gazetteer of New-York.
Henderson's Residence in Iceland.
Ellis's Polynesian Researches.
Capt. Wilkes' U. S. Exploring Expedition.
Baldwin's Pronouncing Gazetteer.

POETRY.

Shakspeare.
Milton's Poetical Works.
Pope's Homer.
Dryden's Virgil.
Thompson's Seasons.
Beattie's Minstrel.
Cowper's Poetical Works.
Young's Poems.
Pope's Works.

MISCELLANEOUS.

Alison on Taste.
Anatomy of Melancholy.
Addison's Works.
Campbell's Philosophy of Rhetoric.
British Prose Writers.
Bacon's Essays.
Beattie's Elements of Moral Science.
Blair's Lectures.
Burke on the Sublime and Beautiful.
Paley's Moral and Political Philosophy.
Burgh's Dignity of Human Nature.

Washington Irving's Works.
D Israeli s Curiosities of Literature.
Diversions of Purley.
Kames Elements of Criticism.
Williston s Eloquence of the United States.
Guardian.
Germany, by Madame De Stael.
Har is Hermes.
Hazlitt's Eloquence of the British Senate.
Locke s Works.
Lacon.
Melmoth's Pliny.
Spectator.
Sismondi s Literature of the South of Europe.
Stewart s Philosophy.
Reid s Philosophy.
Brown s Philosophy.
Dunlop s History of Roman Literature.
Smi h s Moral Sentiments.
Telemachus
Johnson s Works.
Goldsmith s Works.
Phillips, Curran and Grattan.
Cha ham, Burke and Erskine.
Public Instruction in Prussia.
Rush on the Mind.
Seneca's Morals.
Crabbe s Synonymes.
Webster s Philosophical Grammar.
Newman's Rhetoric.
Johnson's Dictionary.
Abbott's Teacher.
Letters to a Student in the First Stages of Education.
Spurzheim's Elementary Principles of Education.
Edgeworth on Practical Education.
Lectures on School Keeping, by Emerson Davis.
Hall's Lectures on School Keeping.
Student's Manual.
Lectures before the American Institute.
Historical Description of the First Public School in Hartford.
Babington on Education.
Education of Children, by John Hall.
Grimke's Reflections on the Objects of Science.
Young Man's Guide.
Wood s Account of Edinburgh Sessional School.
Taylor's District School.
Schoolmaster s Friend and Committee-man's Guide.
Teacher's Guide.
Library of Education.
Manual of Classical Literature.
Combe on Health and Education.
Young Citizen's Manual.
Wayland's Human Responsibility.
St. Pierre's Studies of Nature.
Anacharsis' Travels.
Drake's Essays on the Spectator, &c.
Hints on Education, by Wines.
Cousin's State of Education in Holland.
Simpson on Popular Education.
Crombie's Etymology and Syntax of the English Language.
Means and Ends, or Self-training, by Miss Sedgwick.
Guizot's History of Civilization in Europe.
Couzin's History of Philosophy.

Since the revision of these instructions in 1849, the following are the only works that have been recommended by the Regents:

1850, Feb 14. Webster's Dictionary, as edited by Professor Goodrich, and published by G. & C. Merriam, of Springfield, Mass.
" March 28. Stryker's American Quarterly Register and Magazine.
" Oct. 16. Davies' Logic and Mathematics.
" Oct. 26. The Bible and Civil Government, by Rev. Dr. Matthews.
1851, Oct. 14. Elements of Latin Pronunciation, by S. S. Haldeman.
1852, Feb. 26. The Family and School Monitor and Educational Catechism, by James Henry, Jr.
1853, Jan'y 13. Lossings Field Book of the Revolution.
" June 17. Brodhead's History of New-York.

APPARATUS.

The following articles of philosophical, chemical and mechanical apparatus, &c., are recommended for the use of academies, in the order in which they are enumerated; that is, their relative values, as estimated by the committee, are indicated by the numbers prefixed to them in the list; so that where the funds of an academy will only admit of the purchase of a part of the articles enumerated, those *first* named may be *first* purchased:

1. Globes, terrestial and celestial, Maps, &c.
2. Instruments for Surveying.
3. Air Pump.
4. Chemical apparatus.
5. The Mechanical powers and Hydrostatical apparatus.
6. A Telescope and Quadrant.
7. Electrical apparatus.
8. Orrery and Moveable Planisphere.
9. Numeral frame and Geometrical solids.
10. Tide dial, &c.

VI. Delegation of the powers of Trustees of Academies.

At a meeting of the Regents of the University, held March 31, 1840, Mr. Dix, from the committee to whom it was referred to prepare and submit to the board, the draft of an ordinance defining the conditions on which academies are to receive future shares in the distribution of the income of the Literature Fund, submitted the following report, which the committee deemed proper to accompany the draft of the ordinance prepared by them in obedience to the said reference.

REPORT.

By the annual reports of the academies, on which the last distribution of the income of the Literature Fund was founded, it appears that the trustees of several institutions have rented the buildings erected for their use to particular individuals, for stated purposes, and have surrendered into the hands of such individuals, to a greater or less extent, the management of the affairs of those institutions, in respect to the employment and compensation of teachers and the course of education therein. In most of the cases, in which such contracts have been made, the persons to whom the academic buildings have been leased, have taken charge of them as principals, and have had the general direction of the affairs of the institutions, receiving the fees of tuition and the sum apportioned to them from the income of the Literature Fund, agreeing to sustain any loss arising from the inadequacy of the revenue to the expenditure, and sometimes paying a stipulated yearly rent to the trustees. In some instances, the right of prescribing the course of discipline and study has been surrendered to such persons by the trustees.

The committee consider this practice directly at variance with the design of these institutions, and with the peculiar organization which the law has given them. The trustees are intended as a board for the regulation of all that concerns their internal arrangement, and for the management of their fiscal affairs. Their duties are essentially of a public nature; and it is in view of the public benefits which are expected to flow from the judicious management of these institutions, that they are allowed to participate in the distribution of the public moneys. If they are mismanaged, the trustees should be responsible. Yet, if the academic buildings are leased, and the lessee authorized to employ and regulate the compensation of teachers, and prescribe the course of study, it is manifest that the responsibility of any failure on the part of the institutions to accomplish the objects for which they were created, is virtually transferred from the trustees, their legal managers and guardians, to the lessee, whose private interests may not always correspond with those of the public.

By the Revised Statutes, vol. 1, page 462, sec. 42, (ed. of 1829,) the trustees of the academies are authorized "to direct and prescribe the course of discipline and study in the academy;" "to appoint a treasurer, clerk, principal, masters, tutors, and other necessary officers of the academy; who unless employed under a special contract, shall hold their offices during the pleasure of the trustees;" "to ascertain and fix the salaries of all the officers of the academy, &c."

It appears to the committee that these are trusts which cannot be divested or delegated by those to whom the law has confided them This principle seems to have been settled by the court of chancery in the case of the Auburn Academy, reported in 1 Hopkins, 276. In accordance with this construction of the law, the committee regard all contracts between the trustees of an academy and individuals, by which the power of appointing teachers and fixing their compensation, and of regulating the course of discipline and study in the academy is surrendered, as a violation of their trust, which ought to exclude every such academy from a participation in the annual distribution of the revenue of the Literature Fund. The committee also deem it of the utmost importance that the tuition fees to be paid by students should be fixed by the trustees. Although this duty is not expressly enjoined on them by statute, it results from the nature of their trust, and it cannot be delegated to others consistently with the responsibility of managing the pecuniary concerns of the institution under their charge so as to accomplish the public objects for which it was created. The public moneys annually appropriated for the support of the academies are to be applied to the payment of the wages of teachers. The object of such application is to reduce the rate of tuition fees, and to bring these institutions within the reach of a greater number of persons. This important object may be wholly defeated by surrendering to the principals the right of regulating the charges for tuition, as their interest is to obtain the highest possible rates and thus increase their own compensation. The same public considerations which render it proper for trustees of academies to retain in their own hands the right of fixing tuition fees also dictate that the entire control of the academic buildings should not be surrendered to third persons.

The committee submit the draft of an ordinance in conformity to the foregoing views—(which was duly adopted.)

An Ordinance concerning the Delegation by trustees of Academies to third persons, of the powers conferred on said trustees by law.

The Regents of the University having ascertained from the reports of some of the academies subject to their visitation, that the practice has to some extent existed of renting the academic buildings to third persons as principals, and delegating to them the power of employing teachers, fixing the compensation of such teachers, regulating the charges for tuition, and prescribing the course of study and discipline,

Do ordain and declare,

That all contracts between the trustees of an academy and third persons, which divest the former of their power of controlling the academic building, or by which the right of prescribing the course of discipline and study, of employing teachers and fixing their compensation, or regulating the charges for tuition, is delegated to such third persons, are in violation of the trust with which said trustees are invested by law; and that no academy, the trustees of which shall make such a contract, shall be allowed, during the continuance of the contract, a distributive share of the Literature Fund. But this ordinance is not intended to restrain such trustees from leasing buildings belonging to the academies under their charge, which have been erected or purchased for other purposes than those of study and recitation.

A true copy.

GIDEON HAWLEY,

Secretary of the University.

VII. Incorporation of Select Schools.

I. LAWS OF THE STATE.

For these, see pages 20, 21, of these Instructions.

2. *Ordinance of the Regents respecting the incorporation of Select Schools, adopted May* 4, 1841.

The founders and benefactors of any select school, desiring to have the same incorporated under the sixth article of the first title and fifteenth chapter of the first part of the Revised Statutes, are to make an application for that purpose, to the Regents of the University, in the following manner:

1. The application must be in writing and must be subscribed by as many of the founders as shall have contributed more than one-half of the property collected or appropriated for the use of said school.
2. It must nominate the first trustees, who ought not to exceed twelve in number.
3. It must specify the name by which the corporation is to be called.
4. The property collected or appropriated for the use of the school must be particularly described, with the estimated value of each item, and the property and funds contributed must amount to at least $1,000.
5. The course of study and the system of instruction, intended to be pursued, must be specified.
6. There must be an affidavit annexed to the application by two or more of the applicants, sworn to and subscribed before some officer authorized to take affidavits, to be read in courts of record of this State, stating that the same is made by as many founders of such school as have contributed more than one-half of the property collected or appropriated for its use, and that the facts set forth in the application are true.
7. In case the Regents conceive a compliance with this request will be conducive to the diffusion of useful knowledge, they will declare their approbation of the incorporation of such school.

Under the above law and ordinance, the following incorporation has been made:

June 23, 1851. Hunter Classical School, at Hunter, Greene county.

VIII. Incorporation of Colleges.

I. LAWS OF THE STATE.

See pages 15, 16, and in particular, the law relative to the incorporation of Colleges and Academies, passed April 12, 1853, at page 36.

II. ORDINANCE OF THE REGENTS RESPECTING THE INCORPORATION OF COLLEGES, PASSED JANUARY 9, 1851.

1. When any application is or shall be made to the Regents for the incorporation of a college under the 6th section of the act of the Legislature, passed the 5th day of April, 1813, entitled 'An act relating to the University,' the applicants will be required to satisfy the Regents that suitable buildings for the use of the college will be provided, and that funds to the amount of *one hundred thousand dollars*, with which it is intended to found and provide for such college, have been paid or secured to be paid by valid subscriptions of responsible parties or otherwise.

And in case the Regents shall approve of said application, and the amount aforesaid shall not be invested for the use of said college, either in bonds and mortgages on unincumbered lands within this State, worth at least double the amount so secured therein, or in stocks of this State or the United States, at their market value at the time of the investment, or in the bonds or certificates of stocks legally issued by some incorporated city of this State, at the par value, or in any one or more of the securities above enumerated, a charter shall be granted for the incorporation of such college, for a term of five years, with a condition or proviso therein, that if within the said term of five years the trustees of said college shall present to the Regents satisfactory evidence that they have invested for the use of said college, funds amounting to not less than one hundred thousand dollars, in the manner herein before mentioned, the charter shall be perpetual.

* 2. That in any case in which it shall appear to the Regents of the University, that the state of literature in any academy is so far advanced, that it might be expedient that a president should be appointed for such academy, agreeably to the provisions of the seventeenth section of the act aforesaid; yet the Regents will not in such case, deem the funds of such academy sufficient for such purpose, nor will they in any such case signify their approbation thereof, under their common seal, unless the funds belonging to and held by the trustees of such academy for the exclusive use and benefit thereof shall be proved satisfactorily to the Regents, to be worth at least $130,000, including the fair value of the real estate, the buildings erected thereon, and the funds invested, which may yield a revenue to such academy.

* This 2nd section was originally adopted, May 20, 1836.

III. REPORT OF THE REGENTS OF THE UNIVERSITY ON THE INCORPORATION OF COLLEGES, MADE TO THE LEGISLATURE JANUARY 25, 1853,

The Regents of the University received, on the 1st of April, 1852, a certified copy of the following resolution adopted by the House of Assembly:

"On the application of the New-York Metropolitan College for a charter.

"IN ASSEMALY, *March* 27, 1852.

"*Resolved*, That the general power for incorporating academies, colleges and universities of every description, is sufficiently vested in the Regents of the University, by virtue of the act above recited and the intention of the Constitution of the State; and the said Regents are hereby required to consider the above and all other similar applications for charters now before the Legislature, for medical or literary colleges; and that they be further authorized to revise the ordinances relating to the same, and report such regulations and requisitions for incorporations as they may deem equitable, wise and proper, and calculated to advance the interests of education, science, learning, &c.—said report to be furnished to the Legislature within ten days from the commencement of the next session of the Legislature.

"By order,

"R. U. SHERMAN, *Clerk*."

The Regents, in compliance with the above resolution, have given the subject matter all that consideration which its magnitude and importance require, and now respectfully submit the results of their examination.

The earliest Legislative act, touching the power of incorporating Literary Institutions, was passed on the 1st of May, 1784. It was found, however, to be exceedingly defective, and in a few years gave place to an Act, entitled "*An Act to establish an University, within this State, and for other purposes therein mentioned.*" This law was passed on the 13th of April, 1787, and is now known to have been drafted by Alexander Hamilton. Its leading provisions have been maintained to the present day, and for the sake of convenience of reference, the following section from the Act relative to the University, passed April 5, 1813, may be here quoted:

"*Sec.* 6. *And be it further enacted*, That any citizen or citizens, or bodies corporate, within this State, being disposed to found a College at any place within the same, he or they shall, in writing, make known to the Regents, the place where, the plan on which, and the funds with which, it is intended to found and provide for the same, and who are proposed to be the first trustees; and in case the Regents shall approve thereof, then they shall declare their approbation by an instrument under their common seal, and allow a convenient time for completing the same; and, if at the expiration of the said time, it shall appear to the satisfaction of the Regents, that the said plan and propositions are fully executed, then they shall, by an act under their common seal, declare that the said College, to be named as the founders shall signify, and with such trustees, not exceeding twenty four, nor, less than ten as they shall name, shall forthwith become incorporated, and shall have perpetual succession and enjoy all the corporate rights and privileges enjoyed by Columbia College, in and by the act entitled, An act to institute an university within this State, and for other purposes mentioned therein, passed April 13, 1787."

Under the Act, then, of 1787, (Columbia College having its powers, which had been granted during the existence of the colony of New-York, renewed and enlarged by an Act of the Legislature) the Regents incorporated, from time to time, the following Colleges:

Feb. 26, 1795.—Union College. A previous application for the same, made in 1792, had been refused, on the ground that sufficient funds had not been procured.

May 26, 1812.—Hamilton College. This application was granted on the condition that fifty thousand dollars should be secured, &c.

Feb. 8, 1825.—Geneva College. This charter was granted, on its being shown, that "funds were provided to the extent of sixty thousand dollars, &c."

It is now necessary to state, that during a year intermediate, viz. in 1821, a new Constitution was adopted by the People of the State. This contained a provision in the following words; "The assent of two-thirds of the members elected to each branch of the Legislature, is required to every bill for creating, altering or renewing any body, politic and corporate." It is quite probable, that the incorporation of Geneva College turned the minds of the Legislature of that year, to a consideration of the powers of the Regents as to incorporations. At all events, the Senate requested that body to make "a return of all charters and acts of incorporation granted by them, and of all acts amending, altering or renewing any acts of incorporation adopted by them since the new constitution of this State went into operation; and also requesting them to transmit, at the same time, their views respecting their power to grant acts of incorporation under the new constitution."

The Regents accordingly (Senate Document No. 132, Feb. 18, 1825), made a return of charters and acts of incorporation granted. They further stated, that they were not aware that their power to incorporate Academies and Colleges, was in any manner affected by the new constitution. The proviso above quoted was, manifestly by the terms, confined to the Legislature. And again, the proviso in the 14th Section of the 7th article in words following "nothing contained in this constitution, shall "affect any grants or charters made by this State, or by persons *acting under its authority*," appeared actually to preserve the authority in question, to the Regents.

It does not appear that from this time forward, the power of the regents has been doubted.

With the probably increasing number of applications, the Regents felt constrained to adopt some general rules in these matters, and accordingly on the the 20th of May, 1836, the following ordinance was passed.

"That every future application that may be made by a citizen or citizens, or bodies corporate in this State, to the Regents of the University, for the purpose of founding a college within this State, under the 6th section of the act, passed April 5, 1813, entitled an act relative to the University, shall satisfactorily exhibit to the Regents, that it is the intention of such founder or founders to provide a fund of at least *one hundred thousand dollars* to be invested in bonds and mortgages, on unincumbered real estate, within the jurisdiction of this State, and such investment to continue at least five years from the time of such endowment; such real estate to be worth, at least, by its estimated value, twice the amount of the money so secured thereon; and also to provide for such proposed college, a suitable lot or lots, with a building or buildings erected or to be erected thereon, which shall have cost such founder or founders, at least *thirty thousand dollars*, or which shall reasonably be worth that sum; and that before any ordinance shall be passed by the Regents for a charter to be granted for the incorporation of such college, the Regents shall be satisfied that such endowment has been fully made, agreeably to the provisions of this ordinance."

Until a very recent period (which will be presently stated), the Regents adhered to the terms of this ordinance, and repeatedly denied applications, because its terms were not complied with.

So far as the present examination has extended, it does not appear that the Legislature incorporated any college from 1787 to 1831. From that year to the present, the incorporations by them have been as follows:

April 18, 1831. UNIVERSITY OF THE CITY OF NEW-YORK. (No endowment required as a condition of incorporation.)

April 8, 1836. UNIVERSITY OF WESTERN NEW-YORK, at Buffalo. (No endowment required.)

April 18, 1838. RICHMOND COLLEGE. (No endowment required.)

May 9, 1840. ST. PAUL'S COLLEGE, at Flushing. (No endowment required.)

March 26, 1846. MADISON UNIVERSITY. (No endowment required.)

April 10, 1846. ST. JOHN'S COLLEGE, Fordham. (No endowment required.)

May 8, 1846. UNIVERSITY OF ROCHESTER. (No endowment repuired.)

May 11, 1846. UNIVERSITY OF BUFFALO. (The charter, or statute, contemplates a capital stock of $100,000, and requires a certain amount ($20,000) to be paid in, as necessary for its organization.)

Feb. 27, 1849. GENESEE COLLEGE.. (No endowment required.)

April 17, 1851. NEW-YORK CENTRAL COLLEGE ASSOCIATION, at McGrawville, county of Cortland. (No endowment required.)

April 17, 1851. WESTMINSTER COLLEGE. (No endowment required.)

April 17, 1851. UNIVERSITY OF ALBANY. (No endowment required.)

Jan. 29, 1852. AUBURN FEMALE UNIVERSITY. (No endowment required.)*

On the other hand, from the incorporating of Geneva College to the present date, a solitary application has alone been prosecuted to a successful issue before the Regents. The University of Rochester, apparently unwilling to organize under its legislative charter, applied to the Regents. The earnest desire to comply with the wishes of the petitioners, induced some modifications in the ordinance already recited, and which on the 9th of Jan. 1851, was finally adopted as follows:

Ordinance respecting the Incorporation of Colleges.

The first section of the ordinance respecting the Incorporation of Colleges, passed May 20, 1836, with the additions thereto adopted Jan. 10, 1850, is hereby amended so as to read as follows:

"When any application is or shall be made to the Regents for the incorporation of a college under the 6th section of the act of the Legislature, passed the 5th day of April 1813, entitled 'An act relating to the University,' the applicants will be required to satisfy the Regents that suitable buildings for the use of the college will be provided, and that the funds to the amount of *one hundred thousand dollars*, with which it is intended to found and provide for such college, have been paid or secured to be paid by valid subscriptions of responsible parties or otherwise.

And in case the Regents shall approve of said application, and the amount aforesaid shall not be invested for the use of said college, either in bonds and mortgages on unincumbered lands within this State, worth at least double the amount so secured therein, or in stocks of this State or the United States, at their market value at the time of the investment, or in the bonds or certificates of stocks legally issued by some incorporated city of this State, at the par value, or in any one or more of the securities above enumerated, a charter shall be granted for the incorporation of

* The following have been incorporated since the date of this report:
PEOPLE'S COLLEGE, April 12, 1853, no place named; commissioners appointed to select it.
NEW-YORK STATE AGRICULTURAL COLLEGE, April 15, 1853, no place named.

such college, for a term of five years, with a condition or proviso therein, that if within the said term of five years the trusttees of said college shall present to the Regents satisfactory evidence that they have invested for the use of said college, funds amounting to not less than one hundred thousand dollars, in the manner herein before mentioned, the charter shall be perpetual."

The above ordinance is still in force, and under its provisions, a charter was granted on the 14th of February, 1851, to the *University of Roehester.*

2. Medical Colleges. It is very necessary, not only with reference to the present subject, but also as it regards literary colleges, to be aware, that Columbia College is endowed with all the powers of an university; and by the terms of every successive charter to literary colleges, whether granted by the Legislature or the Regents, similar powers for the establishment of different faculties and the granting of degrees, are substantially conferred. Now it was under these general powers that Columbia College, in former times, appointed a medical faculty, and granted the degree of docter of medicine to candidates who had duly attended lectures, and complied with the other requisitions of the institution.

The *general* power of incorporating Medical Colleges has never been granted to the Regents; but in 1791, the Legislature passed an act to enable them to establish a college of physicians and surgeons in the city of New-York, and the Regents thereupon resolved to establish such a college, and directed a charter to be prepared accordingly. In 1812, a similar act was passed, enabling them to establish a college of physicians and surgeons, at Fairfield, Herkimer county, and a charter was accordingly granted for the same. The first of these is still in existence, and the last is extinct.

The above are the only instances in which the Regents have been authorized to incorporate medical colleges; but the Legislature has repeatedly exercised that authority, as follows:

March 27, 1835. Medical institution of Geneva college. Its degrees of M. D., are declared to be a license to practice.

February 11, 1837. An act authorizing the establishment of a medical faculty in the university of the city of New-York.

Febuary 16, 1839. An act incorporating the Albany Medical College.

May 11, 1846. An act to incorporate the University of Buffalo. A medical department with the usual powers is recognized.

April 8, 1850. An act to incorporate the New-York Medical College.

Let it be observed that these, as well as the Colleges incorporated by the Regents, have the following Statutory Regulations to promote their success. They are each and all endowed by their charters, with the power to grant the degree of *Docter of Medicine*, and which dagree shall be a license to practice. It may be asked, why, if a literary college has University powers and of course can appoint a medical faculty, it has not also the power to grant medical degrees? The reply is, that it can grant such degrees, but the Legislature has ordained (Revised Statutes, Part 1, Title 7, Chap. 14, Sec. 21) that "the degree of Doctor of Medicine conferred by any College in this State, shall not be a license to practise Physic and Surgery." And such an enactment is just and equitable, or else the main object in view in the incorporation of Medical Colleges proper, within the State, might be defeated.

Pending the condition of affairs that has now been stated, another constitution was adopted, which went into operation on the 1st of January, 1847. It altogether ignores the *two-thirds* section previously noticed, and contained the following, which has a very important bearing on the present reference of the Assembly.

Art. VIII. Sec 1. Corporations may be formed under general laws, but shall not be created by special act, except for municipal purposes and in cases where, in the judgment of the Legislature, the object of the corporation cannot be obtained under general laws. All general laws and special acts passed pursuant to this section, may be altered from time to time, or repealed.

The reference of the Hon. the Assembly to the Regents, with the report preceding the same,* is so comprehensive, and in the opinion of this body, presents such correct views, that the labor of enlarging on the subject is necessarily greatly abridged. It is certainly self-evident that the power of incorporation, as exercised by the two bodies, runs counter to each other, and the result is injurious to the best interests of education in the State. Institutions are multiplied, within our borders, as rivals to their predecessors, and with scarcely any requisites to become, what should be their legitimate place, rivals to the literary institutions of other States.

The Regents are therefore ready to recommend that a general law be passed, affirming the power of their body, to incorporate literary colleges, on certain specified conditions; and these conditions they advise should be identical with such as are contained in the ordinance of the 9th of January, 1851, viz: that the sum of one hundred thousand dollars has been paid, or secured to be paid, towards the endowment of the desired college, and furthermore, that suitable buildings have been provided for the use of said college.

That the Regents, in case the above requisitions be not previously complied with, but are satisfied that the subscriptions are sufficiently valid, may grant a provisional charter for the term of *five* years, to enable the applicants to comply with the above requisitions.

That the minor details of the manner of investment, and such further regulations as may be considered necessary, be left with the Regents, with, however, this proviso, that any changes from

* For report, see appendix No. 2.

the terms of the ordinance, passed January 9, 1851, and the enactment now proposed, be duly reported to the Legislature.

As to MEDICAL COLLEGES, the Regents recommend that a general power be granted to them to incorporate the same.

That the charters to be applied for and granted, shall substantially conform to the rules now in force for the incorporation of Literary Colleges.

That every Medical College to be incorporated, shall be subject to the general provisions of the Revised Statutes regulating the practice of physic and surgery within this State, and that annual reports be required to be made to the Regents.

That the sum of fifty thousand dollars, duly invested under such general regulations as the Regents may prescribe, (granting a proper delay, if required, to complete the same) in buildings, museum, library, apparatus, and all other needful appurtenances, be a prerequisite to the incorporation of a Medical College.

That the Regents be authorised to pass general ordinances relating to the faithful government and privileges of all Medical Colleges.

That all Medical Colleges to be hereafter incorporated shall enjoy all the general privileges now granted either by charter or statutory regulations to those now in existence.*

IV. FORM OF THE ANNUAL REPORT OF LITERARY COLLEGES.

(See Revised Statutes as printed in these Instructions, section 39.)

To the Regents of the University of the State of New-York:

The trustees of college, in compliance with a requisition of the Regents of the University, submit the following report for the last collegiate year, ending on the day of containing a just and true statement of facts, showing the progress and condition of said college, during and at the close of said year, in respect to the several subject matters following, viz:

1. *Number and description of Professorships.*

The professorships in said college during said year, as established by the trustees, were the following: (Here state each professorship, as known and defined by the statutes of the college; and if any professorship be vacant, state the fact of such vacancy, when and from what cause it occurred, and whether it is the intention of the trustees to fill the same, and when.)

2. *Faculty and other College Officers.*

The faculty of said college, including all persons charged with the duty of giving public instruction therein during said year consisted of a president, &c. (Here state the number of professors, tutors, &c.)

* An act of the Legislature founded on this report, was passed April 12, 1853, see page 37.

The other officers or servants of said college, charged with duties therein, other than those of public instruction, during said year, were: (Here state the number of such officers, with a description of their office, &c.)

The names of the several persons holding offices or places in said college during said year, with the offices or places held by them respectively, and the salaries or annual compensation for official services, allowed to each of them, were as follows:

Names of persons.	Professorship or other office held.	Salary.

3. *Number of Students.*

The whole number of students, under graduates in said college, during said year, was: (Here state first the whole number of such students, including as well those who left college during said year, as those who remained to the close of it; and including also, as well those, if any, who were received on probation, as those who were regularly matriculated; and then state the number who left college during the year, from any and what cause, if known, with the number remaining at the close of the year; including as well the seniors or graduates of that year, as others.)

The number of graduates at the last annual commencement should then be stated.

The whole number of students in the college at the time of making the report, (if that time be subsequent to the close of the said collegiate year, and after the commencement of the following year,) should then be stated, to enable the Regents to compare present with past numbers, &c.

The number of students (if any) in said college during said year, who were not under graduates, should be here stated, with such description or designation as properly belongs to them.

Under this head, state whether any students in the college during said year, were under the age of fourteen years, and if so, how many; also, what was the average age of the graduates for said year.

4. *Classification of Students.*

The students who were under graduates in said college during said year, were classified as follows, viz: (Here state first the number and names of the classes, and then state the number of students in each class.)

If there be classes in the college under any other than the common designation of Freshmen, Sophomores, Juniors and Seniors, the fact should be particularly stated, with the number and pursuits of the students in such classes.

So also, if there be any students in the college, not coming under the designation of under-graduates, such as students in theology, and law; their classification &c., should be here stated.

5. *College Terms or Sessions.*

The terms or sessions for studies in said college during said year, were the following: (Here state the number of terms, the length of each, when it commenced and ended, and how much vacation there was during said year.

6. *Subjects or Course of Study.*

The subgraduate course of study in each class in said college during said year, was as follows: (Here state the course of each class, beginning with the freshman, for each term in the year, beginning with the first term, designating in each term, *specifically*, the subjects studied by each class, the text books used, and the extent to which each subject was studied, specifying such extent by the number of pages, or proportion of the text book studies, or by other suitable description; and if lectures be given to the class during said term on any subject, designate such subject, with the number and frequency of the lectures on it, and the part or proportion they constitute of a full course of lectures on such subject.)

If subjects of study be pursued in the college which are not subgraduate, either by reason of their not being strictly classical, such as a particular or partial course in mathematics, &c., or by reason of their being superior to a subgraduate course, such as thelogy, law, or medicine, the same designation should be given of the particular subject studied, the text books used, extent of study pursued, lectures, &c., in each class during each term, &c.

7. *Exercises.*

Under this head, state how often the students in the college were exercised during said year, in composition and declamation, in the English language, or in any other and what language, and what criticism such exercises were subjected to; also, whether any other exercises were required of, and performed by them during said year, such as, extemporaneous speaking, or debating, gymnastic, or military exercises, &c.; also, how far exercises in reading or in any other of the primary arts connected with education, were required during said year.

8. *Examinations.*

Under this head state the number of public examinations in the college during said year, when and how long each one was held, and by whom conducted; whether all the classes were examined in all the subjects of study pursued by them subsequent to the last previous examination, if not, what were the omissions and for what cause.

Under this head, state what was the general process of instruction adopted in the college during said year, whether that of *analysis*

9. *Mode of Instruction.*

and recitation from text books, or that of *public lectures*, or *both*, and in what relative proportions. If public lectures were given, state on what subjects, whether the students were required to take notes of them, and what test was applied to ascertain the extent of knowledge acquired by them from such lectures; also, state how often on an average the students were required to recite, or attend lectures.

10. *Discipline.*

Under this head, state the general principles of discipline adopted in the college during said year: what was the general nature of the punishments inflicted; whether any and what discrimination of the relative merits of students was made, either in respect to scholarship or behavior, or both, and what evidence of such merits was preserved or made public.

11. *Gratuitous Aid.*

Under this head, state what provision is made in the college for the gratuitous education of indigent students, or for any other assistance to such students, what number of students during said year were educated in whole or in part, gratuitously, or otherwise assisted, or in any other manner.

12. *Statutes or By-Laws of the College.*

The foregoing form of a collegiate report, requires each college to state in its annual report, specifically, what was ACTUALLY DONE in the college during its last collegiate year, in reference to the most important subject matters of its proceedings during that year.

A copy of the statutes or by-laws of the college, as the same were in force during said year, should be transmitted, with the first collegiate annual report, to be hereafter made to the Regents of the University, that it may be seen what was required by such statutes to be done during said year. But after the first annual report, to be made in pursuance of these instructions, and to be accompanied with a copy of said by-laws, a second copy need not be transmitted with subsequent reports, provided the alterations, if any, in the by-laws first sent, be noted, &c.

13. *Description and Value of College Buildings.*

Under this head, state,

1st. The number, general extent and value of the college buildings and grounds appurtenant thereto.

2d. The number of books in the college library, with their general state of preservation, and estimate of value in the aggregate.

3d. A general description of chemical and philosophical apparatus, &c., belonging to the college, (without designating particulars,) with an estimate of their value in the aggregate.

State the total amount of the above values, to show the whole amount in value, of the college property used as permanent or fixed capital for purposes of instruction, &c.

14. *Description and Value of other College Property.*

Under this head, give a general description and value of the property and funds of the college, other than what is included under the last preceding head, distinguishing real from personal property; and stating the different kinds of personal property, such as bonds and mortgages, bank and other stock, &c., giving the general amount and value of each kind of property; and if any of the college funds be appropriated for any particular purpose, or are required to be kept invested in any particular manner, state the amount of such funds, and whether they are applied to such purpose, or are invested in the manner required.

State in one sum, the total estimated value of all the property described under this general head, after making all proper deductions for depreciation, insufficient securities, &c.

15. *Revenue.*

Under this head, state,

1st. Amount charged for tuition of students in the college during said year, which has been collected or is considered collectable.

2d. Amount charged for room rent of students, use of library, &c., during said year, which has been collected or is considered collectable.

3d. Interest or income of the permanent funds of the college, accrued during said year, which has been collected or is considered collectable.

4th. Income from any other and what source. State in one sum, the total amount of revenue from all the above sources.

16. *Debts.*

State the whole amount of debts contracted by the trustees of the college, and remaining unpaid at the close of the last collegiate year; and if any debts were contracted during said year, state for what cause, or on what account they were contracted, and state also, the amount of interest accrued on said debts for said year.

17. *Income and Expenditures.*

Under this head, compare the whole income of the college, collected or collectable, with its whole expenditures, paid or payable, for said year, to be stated summarily to show how the balance of the account stands.

18. *Price of Tuition, &c.*

Under this head, state the particular prices charged for tuition, for room rent and contingent expenses; also, a general estimate of all other *necessary* annual expenses of a student in said college.

19. *Remarks.*

Under this head, can be stated any remarks which the trustees may have to make on any of the foregoing topics; also, under this head, may be stated, any suggestions which the trustees or faculty of the college may think proper to submit, on any subject connected with their particular institution, or with the general cause of education.

20. *Close of Report.*

As the annual report of the college must hereafter be made by, or under the authority of its trustees (and not as has heretofore generally been done, by the treasurer or secretary alone,) it will be necessary to state, *affirmatively*, at the close of the report, on what authority it is made, &c. If it be made by the trustees at a regular meeting held by them, (which would be the most regular way,) it should be signed by the presiding officer of the board of trustees, for and in their behalf, and the seal of the college should be affixed to it. If the report be made by a committee of the board of trustees, appointed *especially* for that purpose, it should be signed by such committee in behalf of the trustees, and their appointment to make the report should be expresly stated. In either case the treasurer and secretary of the college should subscribe the report, and affix or impress the corporate seal on it, &c.

V. FORM OF THE ANNUAL REPORT OF MEDICAL COLLEGES, OR OF MEDICAL DEPARTMENTS IN LITERARY COLLEGES.

To the Regents of the University of the State of New-York:

The trustees of   college, in compliance with a requisition of the Regents of the University, submit the following report for the last collegiate year, ending on the   day of   containing a just and true statement of facts, showing the progress and condition of said college (or the medical department of said college,) during and at the close of said year, in respect to the several subject matters following, viz:

1. *Number and Description of Professorships.*

The professorships in said college (or in the medical department of said college) during said year, as established by the trustees, were the following: (Here state each professorship, as known and defined by the statutes of the college; and if any professorship be vacant, state the fact of such vacancy, when and from what cause it occurred, and whether it is the intention of the trustees to fill the same, and when.)

2. *Faculty and other College Officers.*

The faculty of said college, (or of the medical department of said college, including all persons charged with the duty of giving public instruction therein during said year, consisted of a president, &c. (Here state the number of professors, tutors, &c.)

The other officers or servants of said college (or of the medical department of said college,) charged with duties therein, other than those of public instruction, during said year, were: (Here state the number of such officers, with a description of their office, &c.)

The names of the several persons holding offices or places in said college, or of the medical department of said college, during said year, with the offices or places held by them respectively, and the salaries or annual compensation for official services, allowed to each of them, were as follows:

Names of persons.	Professorship or other office held.	Salary.

3. *Number of Students.*

The whole number of students, attending the regular course of instruction during said year, was

The number of the graduates of the last annual commencement, was: (Here state when said annual commencement was held.)

The ages of the students attending during said year, were in no case less than 18 years. (If otherwise, state how many were under that age.)

The ages of the graduates being repuired by law to be 21 years, none have been admitted to the degree under that age, and the average age of the graduates at the last commencement, was probably

4. *Classification of Students.*

The students attending said college (or medical department) are classified as follows:

Number attending their first course of lectures,........ ...
" " second course " ....
" " third course " ....
Graduates in medicine,...............................

5. *College Terms or Sessions.*

The term or session for study in said college (or the medical department of said college,) during said year, was the following: (Here state the length of the term.)

6. *Mode of Instruction.*

Under this head, state what was the general process of instruction adopted in the college or of the medical department of said college during said year, whether that of *analysis and recitation from text books*, or that of *public lectures*, or *both*, and in what relative proportions. If public lectures were given, state on what subjects, whether the students were required to take notes of them, and what test was applied to ascertain the extent of knowledge acquired by them from such lectures; also, state how often on an average the students were required to recite, or attend lectures.

7. *Discipline.*

Under this head, state the general principles of discipline adopted in the college or of the medical department of said college, during said year; what was the general nature of the punishment inflicted; whether any and what discrimination of the relative merits of students was made, either in respect to scholarship, or behavior, or both, and what evidence of such merits was preserved, or made public.

Under this head, state what provision is made in the college or of the medical department of said college, for the gratuitous education of indigent students, or for any other assistance to such students, what number of students during said year were educated, in whole or in part, gratuitously, or otherwise assisted out of such funds, or in any other manner.

8 *Statutes or By-Laws of the College.*

The foregoing form of a collegiate report, requires each college to state in its annual report, specifically, what was ACTUALLY DONE in the college during its last collegiate year, in reference to the most important subject matters of its proceedings during that year.

A copy of the statutes or by-laws of the college, as the same were in force during said year, should be transmitted with the first collegiate annual report, to be hereafter made to the Regents of the University, that it may be seen what was required by such statutes to be done during said year. But after the first annual report to be made in pursuance of these instructions, and to be accompanied with a copy of said by-laws, a second copy need not be transmitted with subsequent reports, provided the alterations, if any, in the by-laws first sent, be noted, &c.

9. *Description and value of College buildings.*

Under this head, state,

1st. The number, general extent and value of the college buildings and grounds appurtenant thereto.

2d. The number of books in the college library, with their general state of preservation, and estimate of value in the aggregate.

3d. A general description of chemical and philosophical apparatus, &c., belonging to the college, (without designating particulars,) with an estimate of their value in the aggregate.

State the total amount of the above values, to show the whole amount in value, of the college property used as permanent or fixed capital for purposes of instruction, &c.

11. *Description and value of other College property.*

Under this head, give a general description and value of the property and funds of the college, other than what is included under the last preceding head, distinguishing real from personal property; and stating the different kinds of personal property, such as bonds and mortgages, bank and other stock, &c., giving the general amount and value of each kind of property; and if any of the college funds be appropriated for any particular purpose, or are required to be kept invested in any particular manner, state the amount of such funds, and whether they are applied to such purpose, or are invested in the manner required.

State in one sum, the total estimated value of all the property described under this general head, after making all proper deductions for depreciation, insufficient securities, &c.

12. *Revenue.*

Under this head, state,

1st. Amount charged for tuition of students in the college during said year, which has been collected or is considered collectable.

2d. Amount charged for room rent of students, use of library, &c., during said year, which has been collected or is considered collectable.

3d. Interest or income of the permanent funds of the college, accrued during said year, which has been collected or is considered collectable.

4th. Income from any other and what source. State in one sum, the total amount of revenue from all the above sources.

13. *Debts.*

State the whole amount of debts contracted by the trustees of the college, and remaining unpaid at the close of the last collegiate year; and if any debts were contracted during said year, state for what cause, or on what account they were contracted; and state also, the amount of interest accrued on said debts for said year.

14. *Income and Expenditure.*

Under this head, compare the whole income of the college, collected or collectable, with its whole expenditures, paid or payable, for said year, to be stated summarily to show how the balance of the account stands.

15. *Price of Tuition.*

Under this head, state the particular prices charged for tuition, for room rent and contingent expenses; also, a general estimate of all other *necessary* annual expenses of a student in said college.

16. *Remarks.*

Under this head, can be stated any remarks which the trustees may have to make on any of the foregoing topics; also, under this head may be stated, any suggestions which the trustees or faculty of the college may think proper to submit, on any subject connected with their particular institution, or with the general cause of education.

17. *Close of Report.*

As the annual report of the college must hereafter be made by, or under the authority of its trustees, (and not as has heretofore generally been done, by the treasurer, or secretary alone,) it will be necessary to state, *affirmatively*, at the close of the report, on what authority it is made, &c. If it be made by the trustees at a regular meeting held by them, (which would be the most regular way,) it should be signed by the presiding officer of the board of trustees, for and in their behalf, and the seal of the college should be affixed to it. If the report be made by a committee of the board of trustees, appointed *especially* for that purpose, it should be signed by such committee in behalf of the trustees, and their appointment to make the report should be expressly stated. In either case the treasurer and secretary of the college should subscribe the report, and affix or impress the corporate seal on it, &c.

IX. Instruction of Common School Teachers by Academies.

I. LAWS.

The following abstract of the recent legislation on this subject is here presented, for convenience of reference.

In 1849, the following law was passed.

"The treasurer shall pay, on the warrant of the Comptroller, out of the income of the United States Deposit or Literature Fund, not otherwise appropriated, to the trustees of one or more academies, as the Regents of the University may designate, in each county in this State, the sum of two hundred and fifty dollars per year for the years 1850 and 1851, provided such academy or academies shall have instructed in the science of common school teaching for at least four months during each of said years at least twenty individuals, but no such one county shall receive a larger sum than two hundred and fifty dollars."

(Session Laws 1849, chap. 174, sec. 2. Passed March 30, 1849.)

Under this law the Regents of the University, (see their annual report made March 1, 1850, page 10,) made on the 20th of September 1849 and subsequent, 45 appointments in as many counties.

The return for 1850, (see Annual report made March 1, 1851, p. 227,) shows that 998 common school teachers were instructed during that year.

The return for 1851, (see Annual report of the Regents made March 1, 1852, p. 240,) shows that 1000 common school teachers were instructed during that year.

The next Legislative enactment was as follows:

CHAPTER 536. *An act appropriating the revenues of the Literature and United States Deposite Fund.*

Passed July 11, 1851.

SECTION 4. The Treasurer shall pay yearly, on the warrant of the Comptroller, out of the income of the United States Deposit or Literature Fund, not otherwise appropriated, to the Trustees of one or more academies in each county of the State, as the Regents of the University shall designate, the sum of twelve dollars and fifty cents for each scholar who shall have been instructed in such academy during at least four full calendar months, in the science of Common School Teaching.

Under this law, the Regents of the University at a meeting held Oct 14, 1851, made 87 appointments, (subsequently increased to 90) being two in each county making application for the same.

The return for 1852, (see Annual report of the Regents made March 1, 1853, page 14,) presents the number of 1573 (529 males and 1044 females) thus instructed. A subsequent report from a delinquent academy, increased the number to 1584, (533 males and 1051 females) and the payment by the State was $15,100.

On the 12th of April 1852, the following law was passed (see Session Laws 1852, chap. 235.)

An act to amend an act entitled "An act appropriating the revenues of the Literature and United States Deposite Funds," passed July 11, 1851.

Passed April 12, 1852.

§ 1. Section fourth of the act passed July 11, 1851, entitled "An act appropriating," &c., is hereby amended so as to read as follows:

§ 4. The Treasurer shall pay yearly, on the warrant of the Comptroller, out of the income of the United States Deposite or Literature Fund, not otherwise appropriated, to the Trustees of one or more academies in each county of this State, as the Regents of the University shall designate, the sum of ten dollars for each scholar who shall have been instructed in such academy, during at least one-third of the academic year, in the science of Common School Teaching.

§ 2. This act shall take effect immediately.

In 1853 the following enactments were made.

The act making appropriations for the support of the government, for the fiscal year, commencing Oct. 1, 1853, passed April 13, 1853, (Session Laws 1853, chap. 219, p. 424,) contains the following provision:

"For instruction of Common School Teachers in the academies designated by the Regents of the Universty, eighteen thousand dollars."

Subsequently the following law was adopted:

CHAPTER 402. *An act to provide for the instruction of Common School Teachers.*

Passed June 17, 1853—"three fifths being present."

The People of the State of New-York, represented in Senate and Assembly, do enact as follows:

§ 1. The Treasurer shall pay yearly, on the warrant of the Comptroller, out of the income of the United States Deposite or Literature Funds, not otherwise appropriated, to the trustees of one or more academies in each county of this State, as the Regents of the University shall designate, the sum of ten dollars for each scholar, not to exceed twenty-five scholars to each academy, who shall have been in such academy instructed under a course prescribed by the said Regents, during at least one-third of the academic year, in the science of common school teaching.

§ 2. The Comptroller shall not draw his warrant for any amount as above provided, until the trustees of such academies shall have furnished to the Regents of the University satisfactory evidence that the course prescribed as aforesaid has been thoroughly pursued, by a class previously designated and instructed as common school teachers, and who the said trustees believe intend in good faith to follow the said occupation and shall have obtained a certificate thereof and presented the same to the Comptroller.

§ 3. This act shall take effect immediately.

Under this law, the Regents of the University, at a meeting held July 17, 1853, made 90 *absolute* appointments, being at least two for each county asking the same and 14 *provisional* appointments, that is, if the funds appropriated for the purpose should be found sufficient.

II. FORM OF THE ANNUAL REPORT OR RETURN.

The Regents of the University having under the authority of an act of the Legislature, passed June 17, 1853, designated Academy to instruct scholars in the science of common school teaching, the Trustees and Principal of said Academy do hereby certify and report to the Regents, that during at least one-third of the academic year of said academy, commencing and ending they have accordingly so instructed free of charge, students, of whom were males and females. The names, ages and studies pursued by said students, will be found in the following schedule:

Names.	Ages.	Studies pursued during at least one-third of the academic year commencing
1		
2		
3		
4		

The undersigned further report, that all the students above enumerated have been instructed in the science of common school teaching by

That all have signed a pledge to the effect that they intend to devote a reasonable time to the business of teaching district schools:

That the ages of the students so taught were respectively at the time of their admission, when females, sixteen years or upwards, and when males, eighteen years or upwards:

That additional teacher was employed for the purpose of such instruction:

That the pupils were taught with the other pupils in the academy.

FORM OF AFFIDAVITS.

ss. principal or principal teacher in aca-demy being duly sworn, deposes and says, that the contents of the above report are in all and every part true to the best of his knowledge and belief.

Sworn before

ss. being duly sworn, deposes and says, that he is President, (Chairman, or presiding officer,) of the trustees of Academy, at a legal meeting of which the following named trustees being present, viz:

the above report was presented and approved of by them and ordered to be forwarded to the Regents of the University; and that said trustees, by a resolution entered on their Minutes, declared that the contents of said report were true to the best of their knowledge and belief, and that the course prescribed by the Regents in their circular to academies of the 20th of June, 1853, has been thoroughly pursued by a class as above, previously designated and instructed in common school teaching, and who, the said trustees believe, intend in good faith to follow said occupation.

Sworn before

MEMORANDA.

1. "*One third of the academic year.*" It is understood that in the majority of academies, the *academic year* commences some time during the autumn and ends with the next autumn. It is altogether different from the time to which academies are required to make up their *annual report.* The period of this academic year should be regulated by the by-laws or ordinances of each academy, and this period should be distinctly defined in each report. (See form.)

2. As the great majority of academies have three terms in each year, such at least will have the opportunity to instruct three distinct classes in common school teaching. But if thus divided, this also should be stated in the body of the report, or in a note.

3. The above reports should be engrossed on foolscap paper, with sufficient margin to enable them to be bound, and in letter form, not in the form of law papers.

4. The christian names of students claimed should be given. (Not, for example, C. Andrews, but *Charles* Andrews.) And it would be a great convenience if they were arranged into *males* and *females* separately, and the ages of each sex added.

5. The reports should be transmitted on or before the 1st of January, in the years 1855 and 1856. The general schedule is made up immediately afterwards, and a neglect of any one academy uniformly causes delay, in awarding the monies appropriated.

6. The reports should not be annexed to the annual reports, but forwarded separately.

7. *This Circular should be carefully preserved among the papers of the Trustees.*

X. Miscellaneous.

1. At a meeting of the Regents of the University, held February 14, 1853,

The secretary reported that letters were frequently received from trustees of academies, in which inquiries were made as to the construction of law relative to the powers and duties of said trustees, and their modes of proceeding, and he presented several for the consideration of the board.

After some discussion on the same, it was

Resolved, That it is most proper for this board to decline giving opinions in cases where they are not called to take action in their administrative capacity, and that as a general rule, the secretary be directed to refer to the "Instructions," which contain all the laws and ordinances relative to academies now in force.

2. A law providing for the instruction of common school teachers in academies, was passed July 11, 1851. It made appropriations for *two* years, and by the provisions of our existing constitution, no money could be drawn under it after July 11, 1853. But the academies instructing could not generally complete their instruction at that time.

The following law was accordingly passed :

CHAPTER 299. *An act appropriating the revenues of the Literature and United States' Deposit Funds.*

Passed June 3, 1853.

The People of the State of New-York, represented in Senate and Assembly, do enact as follows:

SECTION 1. The payment to academies for instruction in common school teaching during the academic year eighteen hundred and fifty-three, authorised by the fourth section of chapter five hundred and thirty-six of the laws of New-York, passed July eleventh, eighteen hundred and fifty-one, shall be withheid until after the first day of January, eighteen hundred and fifty-four, and the amount appropriated in said act is hereby reappropriated and then made payable in conformity to existing laws and the ordinances of the Regents.

§ 2. This act shall take effect immediately.

Academies interested should understand that the same difficulty must occur as to the instruction to be given in 1855, as the present law was passed June 17, 1853, and should advise their Senators and members of Assembly accordingly

3. *Ordinance requiring public notice to be given relative to proposed changes in the charters of colleges and academies.* Passed June 10, 1853.

Any college, academy, or institution of learning, desirous of obtaining amendments to, or alterations in its charter, shall give notice of its intended application, to the Regents, for the same, at least six weeks successively, immediately before said application is presented, in a newspaper published at or near the city, town or village in which said college, academy or institution of learning may be situated, and *in the State paper.*

Duly authenticated proof of said publication to be filed with the Regents of the University.

APPENDIX.

I. OBSERVATIONS BY GIDEON HAWLEY, LL.D., LATE SECRETARY OF THE REGENTS, ON CERTAIN BRANCHES OF ACADEMIC INSTRUCTION.

(Reprinted from former Editions.)

In the preceding editions of these Instructions, the Secretary of the University, availing himself of the opportunities they presented for cultivating a more intimate relation, and establishing a more enlarged correspondence with the academies addressed by him, invited the special attention of their trustees and teachers to certain suggestions or inquiries, arranged under the following general heads:

Extent of Elementary Studies.

There is reason to believe that in some academies the elementary branches of education, such as reading and writing, considered as arts, to be perfected by practice, and orthography considered as a subject of knowledge to be acquired by study, are practically, if not avowedly, treated as matters of too humble a rank for academic study; it being understood to be presumed, that such inferior branches of education have been sufficiently attended to in common schools, whose peculiar province it is to instruct in them. And such a presumption must be admitted to be reasonable to a certain extent; as all students who are pursuing subjects of study appropriate for an academy must of necessity have passed through the customary course of a common school education, in which reading, writing and spelling must have formed a necessary part. But it does not therefore follow that these elementary branches of education are not to be any longer cultivated in academies; for whatever proficiency in them may have been made by scholars in the early stages of their education, if their knowledge of them be not kept alive, and matured by repeated exercise during almost the whole period of their minority, they will probably lose much of the benefit of their early acquirements. In this view of the subject, it becomes desirable that the trustees should state in their report, how far exercises in reading, writing and spelling, are required of the higher classes in their academy. The information desired of them can readily be obtained from their teachers, and it is hoped it will not be withheld, either on account of the trouble of procuring it, or any supposed immateriality of it when procured.*

Pronunciation of the English Language.

The trustees or teachers of academies, are also requested to state in their report, under the general head of remarks above referred to, what degree of attention is paid in their academy to the correct pronunciation of the English language, and what standard of pronunciation is adopted by them. If the established rules of pronunciation be taught theoretically, and all errors in the practical application of them, occurring in the ordinary recitations of scholars, and in their daily intercourse with their teachers, be promptly and openly corrected as often as they occur; and especially if such a course be pursued, where it is most needed, in the use of proper names of *persons* and *places*, there is no doubt that every scholar of ordinary aptitude for learning, would in an ordinary course of academic education, acquire a practical knowledge of correct pronunciation, which, growing finally into a involuntary habit, he would carry with him through life. Such an acquisition would certainly be of great value, although if gained in the way here suggested,

* In the Albany Academy, exercises in *spelling* are required as a part of the regular course of study in the lower departments, and as often as at least once a week, in the higher departments. Reading and writing are also particularly attended to, especially the latter; as a good hand-writing, whether considered as a polite accomplishment, or a practical art, increases in value as society advances in civilization and refinement. Considered as an art, the demand for it in this country is already so great, that it will at any time supply to its possessor (in case his other reliances fail him) the place of an actual capital yielding a competent and respectable livelihood. The saving of *time* in reading what is well, compared with what is poorly written, i so great, that it is considered good economy to pay an extra sum for good writing.

it would cost nothing in money, and very little in time; and scholars thus educated would not exhibit (what has sometimes been witnessed in others to the great disparagement of their teachers,) the discreditable contrast of being always able, and sometimes ambitious, to detect the slightest shade of error in quantity or accent of Latin and Greek words, which they will probably seldom, if ever, have occasion to use in after life; while they are unable to detect in others, and commit daily themselves, the grossest errors in the pronunciation of words in their own language of the most daily use.

Subjects of Study.

In respect to the subjects of study proper to be taught in academies, the Secretary, without pretending to claim any right to speak authoritatively, and certainly without wishing to obtrude his own opinion on others, hopes it will not be thought either out of time or place, for him to suggest, that as the current of public sentiment has, for many years, been setting gradually but irresistably in favor of a course of education *more* and *more* practical than any before established, it would be desirable, as it would tend to promote the popular cause of practical education, if the trustees and teachers of academies were to state whether, in the course of instruction established by them, (particularly in reference to students who are not expected to extend their studies beyond the limits of an ordinary academic education,) any, and what, discrimination is made by them, in the various subjects of academic study, between what is *most*, and what is *least practical.**

* To illustrate what is here meant by practical subjects of study, the following re marks are submitted:

The study of Roman antiquities, including whatever of constitutional law Rome possessed, with a minute description of manners, customs, habits, ceremonies, &c., has long been pursued in many of our academies and higher seminaries of learning, and the time commonly spent on them is greater than would be required to study the great principles of our own constitutional law, with selected parts of our civil jurisprudence most applicable to the common concerns of life, such as the formalities required in wills and other instruments, the proceedings necessary to charge endorsers of promissory notes, the statute of limitations, the law of inheritance, the recording act, the common school and highway acts, the right of suffrage and the principles of the election law, with the duties required by law from State, county and town officers, and such other matters as are of like applicability to the daily occurrences in common life. A general knowledge of these latter subjects of study would certainly reward the student with much greater benefits in after life than any thing to be obtained from

The information received from several academies in answer to the preceding inquiries, as well as their own suggestions on the various subjects proposed for their consideration, having subserved the very useful purpose of communicating from one academy to another (through the medium of the published reports of the Regents of the University) any peculiar views entertained, or any special improvements made or suggested by them on the subject of

the study of Grecian or Roman antiquities. Yet it not unfrequently happens that scholars who spend *quarter* after *quarter* in the study of such antiquities, and who are familiar with all their minutiæ, can answer hardly any of the most important questions on our own constitutional law and practical civil jurisprudence. The antiquated constitutions, laws, manners and customs of Greece and Rome, are made subjects of regular study, and cultivated with great assiduity, in several of our academies, while the study of the living practical subjects of our own constitutional law, and the every day occurring principles of our civil jurisprudence, is not admitted as a part of the academic course.

I am not to be understood as intending to disparage the study of Grecian or Roman antiquities, where the student of them is preparing for a liberal education, or aspires to become a man of learning. To such, the study is indispensable; and to all students of the Latin or Greek language, however limited may be their views, the study is proper, as tending to illustrate the authors read by them; and indeed, a general knowledge of the antiquities of Greece and Rome, would be commendable under any circumstances, as it would greatly facilitate the study of Ancient History, and every thing connected with antiquity. But it does appear to me, that the study of our own constitutional law and practical civil jurisprudence, ought to precede, or be concomitant with that of Grecian and Roman antiquities; and for the same reason, that the necessaries of life are first to be secured before its luxuries are to be sought for; and if a student be so restricted in time, that only one of these subjects of study can be attended to, the former should always be *preferred* to the latter; instead of the latter being (as is sometimes the case,) studied to the *exclusion* of the former.

In almost all the higher branches of education taught in our academiess there are parts immediately applicable to the practical purposes of life, while other parts, although not altogether inapplicable to those purposes, are of an abstruse or speculative character; being designed rather to gratify a taste for philosophical or abstract inquiry, than to subserve any very useful or practical purpose. They are all proper subjects of study, without much discrimination, where students have time enough to attend to them, and have already attended to the more practical parts. But students who are restricted in time, as happens probably to a majority in our academies, and whose great object is to acquire knowledge which will best subserve their future purposes of life, should carefully discriminate, or rather their teachers should discriminate for them, between what is practical and what is abstruse or speculative.

To the objection urged against the study of the abstruse or mere speculative part of science, the answer commonly given is, that the object of such study is not so much to acquire useful knowledge as to exercise and improve the understanding of the learner. But this answer, although it meets the objection in part, does not satisfy or education, it occurred to the Secretary of the University, while preparing the last edition of these instructions, that similar inquiries might, with a prospect of similar success, be extended to various other subject matters not less worthy of notice than those already enumerated. The limits, however, necessarily prescribed to him on *that*, as on the *present* occasion, have not permitted such inquiries to be extended beyond one or two topics.

Physical Education.

Education considered in its most extensive sense, that of being a process for improving individuals of the human species, to the full extent of their capabilities, includes physical as well as intellectual or moral improvement. According to the best established theories on the subject, education is held to be properly divisible, and is now commonly divided into three great departments, distinguished in reference to their different subject matters, into *physical*, *moral* and *intellectual*. Of these several departments, the intellectual being considered the most appropriate, if not the most important, for public instruction, has always received, and will doubtless continue to receive in all public institutions, much the greatest share of public attention. Until recently, indeed, in most of our academies, as well as colleges, *intellectual* was cultivated to the almost total neglect of *physical*, if not of *moral* education. But since the principles of Physiology, as applied to the human system, have been more thoroughly investigated, and their value more generally and justly appreciated, *physical education* which depends on the knowledge of such principles, has risen in public estimation to a much higher rank than it formerly held. A knowledge of the laws of *health* or of the means of preserving it, which was once chiefly confined and thought properly to belong to physicians only, has finally found its way into many of our public schools, where it is now cultivated as a regular branch of public instruction.

remove it, for while the fact of such exercise and improvement be not denied, it is equally undeniable that the understanding of a pupil may be as much exercised and improved by studying more useful and practical subjects; and the benefits to him will be thereby doubled; for while he improves his understanding, he stores his mind with useful knowledge.

On most subjects of study, knowledge acquired is as the time bestowed. The same time spent in studying the most worthless, would have served to gain the same amount of knowledge of the most useful. How wise then to bestow our time on the one! how unwise to waste it on the other!

To *cure* disease is admitted to be the *peculiar* office of a physician; and no encroachment on his professional province in that respect is intended or ought to be allowed; but to *prevent* disease, which ordinarily consists only in knowing and obeying the laws of health, or in fulfilling the conditions prescribed for its enjoyment, is not a matter of like professional or exclusive *monopoly.* Nor is it so considered by physicians, many of whom are among the most strenuous advocates for making Physiology, and particularly that part of it which relates to the laws of health, or the means of securing and preserving the human system in its best possible condition, a subject of regular study in all our institutions for public instruction. And so general has public sentiment now become in favor of such a study, that nothing but a want of suitable text books has prevented its general introduction into our public schools.

In view of such considerations, it becomes desirable to ascertain what degree of attention is paid in any of our academies to physical education, considered with special reference to health, or to the best possible development of the corporal or animal functions. The trustees or teachers of academies are therefore requested to communicate in their future reports to the Regents, the information desired on the subject above proposed, particularly in as far as it relates to ventilation of school rooms; corporeal position of scholars in school, and gymnastic or other exercises out of school, &c.

The teachers of some academies, while professing to furnish the information as above requested, have described the peculiar advantages, or facilities, for ventilation which their school rooms possessed, without stating the important fact, whether and how they practically avail themselves of such advantages or facilities. That it may be seen what importance is attached to such matters elsewhere, the following extract from the regulations or instructions established for the government of a normal school of distinguished celebrity at Edinburg, is subjoined:

"Great attention should be given to the ventilation of school rooms, so that on no account, even for a few minutes, their inmates shall breathe bad air. The privileges and advantages of ventilation must be dwelt on; the temperature of school rooms must be attendedto; there must be no constrained posture either in standing or sitting; no injury to the spine by want of back support in sitting; and no confinement for more than an hour at a time without exercise in the open air, with the benefit of rotary swings and other safe gymnastics; rooms when empty, to be well aired by cross windows; and such airing to be repeated hourly when practicable."*

These regulations are minute, and may at first view appear unimportant; but not so, it is believed, after further reflection. The importance of ventilation, especially, cannot well be overrated. It is a subject which has recently attracted much public attention, both in this and in other countries, and it is now undergoing a course of investigation and discussion, which is expected to lead to the most beneficial results.

Fxtent of Study Memoriter, or by Rote.

To suffer a pupil to learn the demonstration of a mathematical theorem by *rote*, which is a mere artificial drill on the memory,

* In the Albany Female Academy the trustees, some years since, established the following regulations on the subject of ventilating their school rooms, which have ever since been strictly enforced, and with the most beneficial results; "It shall be the duty of the steward to see that the whole academy edifice be kept at all times ventilated in the best practicable manner, and to secure such ventilation, which the trustees consider of the first importance, it is hereby made the special duty of the steward (until a suitable ventilator through the ceiling and roof, above the upper hall, shall be constructed,) to lower or cause to be lowered, after the exercises of each day shall be closed, as well in the winter as in the summer season, an upper sash of one or more of the windows in each of the rooms in the academy which shall have been occupied during the day, and to cause the same to be kept so lowered during the summer season for the whole night, except in rainy, or other unsuitable weather, and in other seasons of the year to cause the same to be kept so lowered for at least an hour each day, and at all times, when the weather will permit, to keep the upper sash of one or more of the windows in the chapel (being an upper room) down both night and day, and also to keep, during the day time in the summer season, and whenever the weather will permit in other seasons of the year, the front or outward door, opening into the lower hall, open, by fastening the same back, and also to keep one of the sashes in the windows of the halls above, either up or down, so as to admit of the constant entrance of fresh air."

It is proper to state in connection with the subject of the above note, that the trustees of the same academy have established a regulation on another subject which they consider of equal importance—that of providing seats with backs, so that no pupils in their academy shall be permitted to sit without suitable *back* supports. The object of such a regulation is too obvious to require explanation, and it is hoped that it only requires to be presented to the notice of trustees and teachers to secure its adoption in all our academies. G. H.

without the exercise of the understanding, would be condemned as *absurd.* On the other hand, to require a pupil, in adding or multiplying numbers in arithmetical operations, to rely on his understanding solely, without any aid from artificial memory, in the use of addition or multiplication tables, would be equally *absurd.* Hence it is plain that *some* subjects of study must be addressed chiefly to the understanding, while *others* require only the aid of memory. To the former class, belong all conclusions drawn by reasoning from pre-established premises, whether on moral, mathematical, or physical subjects. And of a kindred, although not of the same character, are all such matters as being connected by certain affinities, may when once learned in that connection, be recalled to mind by a principle of association, which in such cases supplies the place of artificial memory. To the other class, that of things requiring to be learned by rote, belong all isolated facts as well as ultimate principles. And if, for the purpose of securing a more ready command over them, we treat as belonging to the same class, many facts not wholly isolated, as well as many principles not strictly ultimate, we shall probably find it tend much more to effect our object, than to depend for their remembrance in time of need, on the uncertain power of recollecting them from their relations to other things; for it will be found that in proportion as such facts and principles have been learned by rote in early life; so will commonly be their subserviency to practical purposes in after life. Let any one of mature age undertake to estimate the value of having a ready command over such facts and principles, and, unless his early education shall have been different from the common course, he will regret that his store of them is not more abundant; and if it were possible for him to recall and revise what is past, it cannot be doubted, that to enlarge that store would be among the first acts of his revision. How many matters once well understood in their *rationale*, but long since forgotten, he would make the subjects of study by rote, reiterating their impression on his memory for the same reason, if not to the same extent, as in early life he did the common addition and multiplication tables, or the common rules in grammar and arithmetic. How industrious would he be in treasuring up for future use, such matters as the specific gravity of bodies, their constituent parts and proportions, with other like important truths in chemistry and physics—the leading dates and events in history, topographical statistics, with many other matters alike important for future reference. Nor would he, in laying up such a store of knowledge, fail to include in it some of the leading principles of science; such for example, as the universal law of gravity—*attraction directly as quantity of matter and inversely as the square of the distance*; or the law of falling bodies—*spaces described as the squares of the times*; or the fundamental principle in mechanics—*equality of products from moving power and resisting weight multiplied each into its own velocity*; or separately—*momentum, as quantity of matter multiplied into its velocity*: and such also as the important law of fluids—*pressure as depth independent of breadth, with resistance to moving bodies as the square of their velocities*; or as such as the sublime discovery in astronomy, *planets all moving in elliptical orbits, each describing equal areas in equal times, with the squares of their periodic times as the cubes of their mean distances from the sun.* How greatly to be desired would be a knowledge of such principles always at command; and yet if we depend for our knowledge of them, on having once demonstrated them, how frail will be the dependence! how transient the knowledge! While on the other hand, if such knowledge be artificially impressed on the memory, like that of other things learned in early life by rote, how lasting it becomes! The demonstration of the principle may long since have been forgotten, but the principle itself will remain.

From a course of remarks similar to the above, in the last edition of these Instructions, it was, as I have been informed, inferred by some under whose notice the remarks happened to fall, that the writer of them intended to recommend study by rote, in preference to study by demonstration; thus exalting the faculty of memory to the debasement of that of the understanding. And it must be admitted that from certain unqualified expressions inadvertently used on that occasion, such an inference would seem to be in some measure warranted. But no such inference was intended or foreseen. The writer would hope to be among the last to disparage intelligent study, or to enlarge the province of memory by encroaching on that of the understanding. The only position intended to be taken by him was simply this—that there are many principles, which being once learned from demonstration ought to be afterwards inculcated by rote, not that they were to be *originally* learned in that way, but only so inculcated *after* first being demonstrated in the ordinary way.

The position thus qualified and explained is still maintained, and may, I think, be easily defended. Let us illustrate it by a few practical cases. Suppose it be required to compute the superficial areas of different figures; how important to have at command the principles on which the computation depends; such as the area of a parallelogram being equal to the product of its base into its altitude—of a triangle to one-half such product—of a circle to the product of one-half its radius into its circumference, and of a sphere to four times that product. So if we wish to compare the areas of different figures, how desirable to know that the areas of all similar figures are as the squares of their corresponding or homologous sides—or if it be required to compute the solid contents of bodies, how convenient to be able to apply at once the principles of the computation—such as a cone being one-third of a cylinder of the same base and altitude—a sphere two-thirds of a cylinder circumscribed around it and having the same altitude—with innumerable other cases of a similar character. Or if we change the field of illustration from geometry to physics, we shall find equally striking instances of the same general truth; such for example as the case of a traveller desirous to measure the depth of a precipice, on the top of which he stands. How important, for that purpose, that he should know without recourse to books, that if he throw down a stone it will fall sixteen feet the first second, forty-eight the next, and so on—the spaces described being always as the squares of the times of descent; so that if he have with him a watch beating seconds, or for want of that, if he refer to the beating of his own pulse, in an ordinary state, he can ascertain with sufficient accuracy the depth of the precipice to be measured. Again, if we are acquainted with the specific gravities of different bodies, and have the knowledge so stored in the memory as to be always available, how convenient it would be for practical application in estimating the weight of stone, iron, &c. Or to be more particular, suppose a traveller wishes to ascertain the height of a mountain he is about to ascend. If he has had the good fortune to learn and retain in memory, the specific gravity of mercury and atmospheric air, he will, on comparing them, find the former about 12,000 times heavier than the latter, from which he will at once infer that one inch of mercury is equal in weight to 12,000 inches of air—or in other words, that a fall of one inch in his barometer indicates an ascent of 12,000 inches, or 1,000 feet, up the mountain.

To illustrate the value of knowledge at command, I will only refer to one other case, that of ascertaining heights and distances from the sphericity of the earth. A single mile of even surface, such as that of water, curvates from a straight line drawn as a tangent to that surface eight inches—two miles, thirty-two inches—three miles, seventy-two inches, or six feet; the curvation being, for moderate distances, as their squares, or nearly so. Hence if we are acquainted with the simple principle here stated, we may measure heights by distances, and distances by heights, with only one of them given or ascertained; and if our knowledge of the principle be always at command, how convenient it would be for practical use when a ship at sea first discovers the top of a mountain, light-house, or other object of *known* elevation; for by knowing its elevation, its distances may be at once ascertained; so if the distance be known the elevation of the mountain may be in the like manner ascertained.

The principle involved in all the cases referred to in the preceding remarks in defence of the position there assumed, ought I admit, to be demonstrated so far as it may be demonstrable, by every student, on his first undertaking to learn it; and he should be kept to the demonstration until he fully comprehends it. But after that be done, I hold, and have in the preceding remarks endeavored to show, that the principle itself without the demonstration should be inculcated on the memory in the same manner as if it were to be learned only by rote. Demonstrations in their best form are too complex, and in their common form too artificial to be long retained in memory; but principles, abstracted from their demonstrations, and expressed with suitable concentration of thought and language, are not more difficult to be learned and retained by rote, than most other things which it is common to learn and retain in that way. Take for example the principle involved in one of the cases above referred to, that of measuring heights and distances from the sphericity of the earth. The demonstration of the principle would occupy considerable time, and require much thought, but the principle itself may be concentrated almost to a point, such as—*the surface of the earth curvates from any given point, according to the square of the distance, being for a single mile eight inches.* The *demonstration* of such a principle, it would be difficult for most persons to retain long in memory, but the principle itself being once learned by rote, nothing would be easier than to retain it; it would indeed remain of itself, like every thing else which becomes habitual or involuntary.

The chief object of the preceding remarks is to present for the consideration of academic teachers, what is thought to be an important subject, and to invite them in their future reports, to communicate as mere matter of fact, how far the mode of instruction pursued by them is in accordance with the principles involved in these remarks.*

* The writer of these instructions intended at first to present, for the consideration of academic teachers, another subject—that of *composition*, considered as a scholastic exercise; but having already reached, if not gone beyond, the limits prescribed to him, he is prevented from executing his first intention. He can not, however, forbear to present, in the most unpretending form, that of an appendix *note*, a few brief suggestions on the subject above referred to.

Composition is an exercise requiring two different operations of the mind—originating or carrying on a train of thought, and expressing it in language. How intimately these operations are connected, and how wonderfully they act and react on each other, it is not here proposed to inquire; all I propose now to do is to offer a few remarks on composition, considered in reference merely to *language*.

Language, in whatever point of light it may be considered, resolves itself ultimately into the use of outward signs for expressing inward thought or feeling; words being nothing but signs, and their meaning the things signified. In reading printed, or hearing spoken language, which is more or less the daily occupation of almost every person, we are constantly passing from the sign to the thing signified, from words to their meaning; and hence we become so familiar with their connection in that order where the sign is first presented, and the mind always passes from that to the thing signified—that we are never embarrassed in the ordinary exercise of reading written, or hearing spoken language. A man of common education will read a common English book a whole day, without being at a loss for the meaning of a single word in it. The reason undoubtedly is, that during his early education, it was his daily practice to learn, and in after life to apply words and their meaning in the order in which they are always presented in *reading*. But how immeasurably different with the same man (supposing him to be of the ordinary class,) is the same exercise when reversed —that is, when he is required to pass from the *thing* signified to the *sign*—from thought to language or expression—which constitutes the whole exercise of composition, as we are now considering it. He hesitates—is embarrassed—and at a loss every step he takes; not because he is ignorant of the meaning of words, or of their connection, considered as signs, with thought, as the thing signified; but because he is not familiar with that connection presented in that order, where the idea or thing signified comes first, and the word or sign of it last. Only give him the sign first, and he passes instantly to the thing signified, because he is daily accustomed to such an operation—to seeing words or hearing sounds, and connecting them with their appropriate meaning.

To show how much depends on the order in which we are accustomed to learn things, we have only to refer to our knowledge of the common alphabet, where we shall find every thing depending on the order in which its letters have been learned. If we repeat them in their accustomed order, we run through them with the greatest ease and rapidity; but on reversing that order and attempting to repeat the letters backwards, we meet with the greatest embarrassment; and yet there is nothing in the nature of the letters making them easier to learn or repeat in one order than in another. Each order is in itself arbitrary—for if we make ourselves as familiar with the letters in their reversed as in their direct order, we find it as easy to say them backwards as forwards. And so it is with language, if we can make ourselves as familiar with the connection between words and ideas, in the reversed as in the direct order, we shall find as little difficulty in passing from one to the other, in one order as another.

Since then so much depends on the order in which we are accustomed to consider words and ideas, it would seem to be reasonable to conclude that in proportion as we become familiar with that order, as it always occurs in composition, will be our facility in composing—and that if we can become as familiar with the exercise of composing for ourselves, as we are with reading what is composed by others, we may (having reference only to language) perform one operation as easily as the other. Assuming such a conclusion to be well founded, how can we best accomplish so desirable an object—that of making ourselves as familiar with composition as with reading? Shall we require more frequent exercises in composition, in which the student is always first required to find ideas, and then signs or words to express them? That would tend directly to accomplish the object; and where there is no want of ideas, and no reluctance to undertake the written expression of them, no better means of accomplishment can be used. But are such means *ordinarily* the best that can be applied? The youthful mind is commonly more reluctant to engage in exercises of composition, than in any thing else required to be done. And why is it so? They who have no want of ideas, and know how to express them, feel no such reluctance. On the contrary, they are often ambitious to give body and form to their conceptions, either in written or spoken language. The reluctance then must proceed either from paucity of ideas, or inability to express them—from want of thought or ignorance of language, or from both causes combined. The latter is probably the most common source of the reluctance, and we shall accordingly so consider it. The question then arises, what are the best means of supplying such defect or want of thought, and of imparting the requisite knowledge of language? Without undertaking to enumerate all the means that may be used for such a purpose, I will only here specify two of them—*translation* from a dead or foreign language into our own —and *analysis* of English text books. These I consider to be the most leading and important means, not only to remove the reluctance above noticed, and thereby to gain *indirectly* the principal end above proposed, but also to subserve that end *directly.* This may, I think, be shown by the following summary views, which might be greatly amplified, if time and space would permit.

In translating from another into our own language, the first step in the process is to find out the thought or idea to be translated. When that is done, the next step is, *or at least should be*, to find English words best fitted, and to collate or arrange them in the order best calculated to express the translated idea, according to the true spirit or idiom of the English language. Here then we have an operation directly the reverse of that which occurs in reading from our own language. Instead of passing from words to ideas—from the sign to the thing signified, which is all that we do in reading—we do, in the exercise or act of translation, necessarily pass from ideas to words—from the thing signified to the sign, thus becoming as familiar with their connection, when viewed in the *reversed*, as we were before in the *direct* order. Now such a *reversed* view is what is always required to be taken in every exercise in composition; and in proportion to our familiarity with such a view, will be our facility in composing. In short, to sum up the whole matter in the fewest possible words, *translation* from one language into another is, in respect to its influence on the power of expressing thought in the language to which it is converted a continued process of composition *in* the latter language. It is not merely equivalent to such a process, but is such a process itself. *Here* then probably lies the chief, or one of the chief benefits derivable from the study of the Latin and Greek languages. They furnish the most abundant and variegated store of ideas, and at the same time the collocation of their words is so radically different from ours, that the translation of them into our own language serves the purpose of improvement in English composition, in the same manner and to the same extent, as the exercise of clothing or expressing an original idea in its appropriate English language.

In view of this latter source of benefit from the study of Latin and Greek, what are we to think of the practice, tolerated, if not encouraged in some of our academies, of allowing students in those languages to consult *ad libitum*, translations of the books read by them? What else *can* we think of it, than that it tends to defeat one of the chief and most rational objects that can be proposed in such a study—that of improving the inventive faculty in the expression of thought? How much less irrational is it, than to give to a student a subject for his exercise in composition, and then to write it out for him? What is it, in short, but giving him at once both a sign and the thing signified, without requiring or allowing any exercise of his own faculties? But although we might greatly enlarge on this topic, our limits, both in time and space, forbid its further prosecution. We have only room to add a very few remarks on the exercise of analyzing text books.

The analysis of English text books may be so conducted, as to subserve the purposes of improvement in English composition, in much the same manner, and for the same reasons, as translation from a foreign language into our own. The text book furnishes a train of thought, expressed in language more or less peculiar to each author, and if the student be required to express the same thought in his own language, to borrow only the author's ideas, but not his words, he will necessarily exercise his mind in finding signs or words for ideas—that is, in passing from the thing signified to the sign, in much the same manner as if he were translating a foreign into his native language, or clothing an original idea in its appropriate words. If such be a correct view of the case, how much to be condemned must that practice or mode of instruction be, which allows a student, in analyzing a text book, to use in all cases the language of its author, or which does not admonish him of his error, when he does so use it.

G. H.

II. REPORT OF THE COMMITTEE ON COLLEGES, ACADEMIES AND COMMON SCHOOLS AGAINST GRANTING A CHARTER TO THE METROPOLITAN COLLEGE.

(Referred to at page 104.)

The committee on colleges and schools, to which was referred the application for an incorporation of a college by the title of "The New-York Metropolitan Medical College," report:

That there are at present within the bounds of the city of New-York three regularly incorporated Medical Colleges: "The College of Physicians and Surgeons in the city of New-York," "The Medical Department of the New-York University," and "The New-York Medical College;" the charters of Columbia, Union and Hamilton Colleges also allow those institutions to erect medical departments whenever it may be deemed expedient; that in addition to these there are within the State the following medical incorporations: "The Albany Medical College," "The Medical Department of Geneva College," and "The Medical Department of the University of Buffalo." The committee further report that all and each of these are at present, or have been during the last three years, applicants for the bounty of the State. The only exception to this statement that can, with any semblance of truth, be offered, is that probably some may not have presented formal petitions for relief; but it is perfectly well understood that such is the intention and wish of all provided the Legislature appear disposed to listen favorably to the wishes of a single one.

The debts of these institutions, as formally reported to the Regents of the University in 1851, were:

College of Physicians and Surgeons, N. Y.,			$15,000
Medical Department of Geneva College,			400
do	do	New-York University,	47,000
do	do	Buffalo University,	3,300
Total,			$65,700

No statement is made by the New-York Medical College, but it is quite probable that the buildings and apparatus are private property; at all events here are four of the six Medical Colleges of the State, after being in existence for a greater or less period of time, burthened with a debt of sixty-five thousand dollars, and one, or more, or all of them annually asking for assistance of the Legislature. The same state of things exists in our literary colleges, and we fear will continue to exist while the Legislature, instead of

" strengthening the things that are ready to perish," regard with favor each and every application for a charter. Should such an evil be continued and encouraged, will it be checked by continually adding to the number of the incorporated institutions of the State? Is it enough that the design is laudable, the petitioners respectable, the object they have in view praiseworthy? With more justice and greater propriety does it become the Legislature to deliberate whether the wants of community require the multiplication of institutions ostensibly devoted to the higher branches of literature, science or the arts. If the simple increase in the number of literary and scientific institutions in the State elevated the standard of education or reduced the expense incurred in securing the same, no objection would be raised by the committee to this or any other kindred application. If the present incorporated colleges of the State fail to fulfil the obligations and requirements imposed upon them by their charters, let them be anulled; if not why incorporate more rivals who, in turn, will seek for " aid and comfort" from the treasury of the State? With six medical and nearly double the number of literary colleges in this state, the idea of a monopoly in the business of education is an absurdity, while at the same time no obstacle is thrown in the way of any body of men securing charters from the Regents for as many such institutions as they may desire without the aid of legislative intervention. Last year no less than three colleges received charters from the Legislature; this year the number of applicants has increased to five or six. Is it not time that this system of legislation should cease? Are the people of the State ready to increase the annual amount awarded to these institutions in equal ratio to their rapid annual increase? Or, if the fund remains permanent, is it to be divided and sub-divided until each one shall receive an infinitesmal share? It is now nearly forty years ago (1813) since the Legislature empowered the Regents of the University to incorporate *literary* colleges under such restrictions as might seem expedient. That power is possessed by them at the present time; but it has been the plan adopted by different applicants for various charters to resort to the Legislature for aid, and hence charter after charter has been granted to new institutions; institutions freed from the wholesome and judicious restraints imposed upon those chartered by the Regents. The charter is granted one year, the next they are " knocking at the door" of the halls of legislation for a portion of the bounty of the State; so pressing are the wants of some of them, that the same Legislature that gives them their chartered rights and privileges are requested to endow them, an example of which we have at the present session, when scarcely a month intervenes from the request to give us a charter to that of give us $50,000 " in two years from date." It does appear to the committee that, sooner or later, it will become the imperious duty and desire of the Legislature to leave the consideration of these matters with those whose duties, powers and obligations have special reference to matters pertaining to academies and colleges. The committee would also suggest that a slight amendment be made in the Act of 1813 relative to the University, to wit: inserting the words "literary and medical" before "colleges" in the sixth section. This would confer all the necessary power upon the Regents of the University. To this should be added a general law for the incorporation of colleges and universities of all descriptions, to meet which, if in the spirit and tenor of the rule adopted by the Regents, would, it is presumed, check many of the applications now pressed upon the Legislature.

There seems to exist an honest difference of opinion in the minds not only of legislators, but of our fellow citizens generally, as to what extent the State is bound in good faith, and mere policy to aid and assist in sustaining the higher branches of education as taught in our colleges. Some are far more liberal in their views than others while others would take away all public patronage; but in the matter of creating or bolstering up poor or worthless institutions, or such as are likely to be a State charge, there can be no question or doubt on the subject. If, then, we would not render those in operation still less able to sustain themselves than they are now, why increase their difficulties by adding to their numbers and increasing the tax for their support.

It may with propriety be asked why so many of our youth of New-York seek for a liberal education in other States? Is it because we have not enough of colleges? or has the educational corps of instructors, divided up into nearly a dozen of colleges, failed in erecting thrifty and popular institutions, which would not only have retained the sons of the State, but have drawn many students from abroad had their efforts been concentrated in two or three colleges? True, some aspiring village or third rate town might have lost a few dollars by such a change; but the interests of education and the treasury of the State would both have been gainers by the operation.

It may with great propriety be asked, why impose upon colleges incorporated by the Regents certain obligations and restrictions that are not imposed upon those chartered by the Legislature? If a wise policy, the experience of years, confirms and strengthens the opinion that these restrictions and requirements are proper, just and equitable, why should any favoritism and partiality be shown to one in preference to another. The true friends of learning are not opposed to colleges or universities, academies or lyceums; they belong to and cannot, without violence to the best interests of science and learning, be separated from our educational course, the first step of which is taken in the common school; but, in commercial language, "the market is overstocked."

Your committee believe that the real difficulty in regard to colleges is not sufficiently understood, certainly not appreciated. It is a want of *qualified teachers* to fill the posts of honor and responsibility to which they are called. In the formation of these new faculties, the wants and poverty of some of these institutions compel them to take inferior instructors, so that now, it is no uncommon thing, we learn, for those appointed to certain departments to qualify themselves after they have been elected to perform the functions and duties of their stations.

If, then, the standard of professorship is deteriorating *by this rapid multiplication of colleges*, it must follow as a natural consequence that the opportunities of the student, and his advance in knowledge, must suffer a like injury.

It has ever been the policy of the State of New-York to assist in sustaining her institutions of learning. One of these, by means of this assistance, has already opened wide her doors as a free college to all who wish to enter; two others are, we believe, free from want, and neither have asked, desire or seek for further aid from the State. The younger and feebler institutions now seeking for assistance are, we believe, all of them worthy and entitled, and we trust will receive the bounty of the State. Do they not, in connection with our medical colleges present number and variety enough for the choice of the most fastidious? Believing that neither the wants of the community, or the interests of science, require the incorporation of the Metropolitan College in the city of New-York; the minority of the committee on colleges and schools *Resolve*, That the prayer of the petitioners be denied. They also offer the following amendment, which, if adopted, would relieve the Legislature from much embarrassment and sound learning from much reproach:

An act relative to the University, passed April 5th, 1813, is hereby amended by inserting before the word "college," (see section 6 or 1,) at the commencement of the first sentence, "*literary, medical or both.*" The sentence amended would read as follows:

That any citizen or citizens, or bodies corporate within this State, being disposed to found a literary or a medical college, or both, &c.

They would also offer the following resolution and move its adoption:

Resolved, That the general power for incorporating academies, colleges and universities of every description is sufficiently vested in the Regents of the University by virtue of the act above recited and the intentions of the Constitution of the State; and the said Regents are hereby required to consider the above and all other similar applications for charters now before the Legislature for medical or literary colleges; and that they be further authorised to revise the ordinances relating to the same and report such regulations and requisitions for incorporations as they may deem equitable, wise and proper, and calculated to advance the interests of education, science, learning, &c., said report to be furnished to the Legislature within ten days from the commencement of the next session of the Legislature.

III. CATALOGUE OF ACADEMIES

Incorporated by the Regents of the University to the 1st of January, 1854, arranged according to the date of their incorporation.

NAMES.	Town.	County.	Date of incorporation.	Remarks.
1. Erasmus Hall	Flatbush	Kings	November 17, 1787.	
2. Clinton Academy	East-Hampton	Suffolk	November 17, 1787.	
3. North Salem Academy	North-Salem	Westchester	February 19, 1790.	
4. Farmers' Hall	Goshen	Orange	March 26, 1790.	
5. Montgomery Academy	Montgomery	Orange	January 21, 1791.	
6. Washington Academy	Salem	Washington	February 15, 1791.	
7. Dutchess County Academy	Poughkeepsie	Dutchess	February 1, 1792.	
8. Union Hall	Jamaica	Kings	February 29, 1792.	
9. Hamilton Oneida Academy	Whitestown	Oneida	January 29, 1793.	Merged in Hamilton College.
10. Schenectady Academy*	Schenectady	Schenectady	January 29, 1793.	
11. Oxford Academy	Oxford	Chenango	January 27, 1794.	
12. Johnstown Academy	Johnstown	Fulton	January 27, 1794.	
13. Kingston Academy	Kingston	Ulster	February 3, 1795.	
14. Canandaigua Academy	Canandaigua	Ontario	March 4, 1795.	
15. Union Academy	Stone Arabia	Montgomery	March 31, 1795.	Extinct.
16. Otsego Academy	Cooperstown	Otsego	February 8, 1796.	Extinct.
17. Cherry Valley Academy	Cherry-Valley	Otsego	February 8, 1796.	
18. Lansingburgh Academy	Lansingburgh	Rensselaer	February 8, 1796.	
19. Columbia Academy	Kinderhook	Columbia	March 13, 1797.	Extinct.
20. Cayuga Academy	Aurora	Cayuga	March 23, 1801.	
21. Fairfield Academy	Fairfield	Herkimer	March 15, 1803.	
22. Oyster-Bay Academy	Oyster-Bay	Queens	March 15, 1803.	

* No 10. Schenectady Academy having been supposed to be merged in Union College, it was revived by an act passed April 17, 1818. See also an act passed April 25, 1831.

CATALOGUE OF ACADEMIES.—(CONTINUED.)

NAMES.	Town.	County.	Date of incorporation.	Remarks.
23. Catskill Academy	Catskill	Greene	March 12, 1804.	Extinct.
24. Newburgh Academy	Newburgh	Orange	March 3, 1806.	Extinct.
25. Hudson Academy	Hudson	Columbia	March 3. 1807.	
26. Lowville Academy	Lowville	Lewis	March 21, 1808.	
27. Ballston Academy	Ballston	Saratoga	March 21, 1808.	Extinct.
28. Pompey Academy	Pompey	Onondaga	March 11, 1811.	
29. Washington Academy	Warwick	Orange	March 25, 1811.	Extinct.
30. Blooming-grove Academy	Blooming-grove	Orange	April 1, 1811.	Extinct.
31. Albany Academy	Albany	Albany	March 4, 1813.	
32. Whitesborough Academy	Whitesborough.	Oneida	March 23, 1813.	
33. Geneva Academy	Geneva	Ontario	March 29, 1813.	Merged in Geneva College.
34. Onondaga Academy	Onondaga	Onondaga	April 10, 1813.	
35. Utica Academy	Utica	Oneida	March 14, 1814.	
36. Auburn Academy	Auburn	Cayuga	February 14, 1815.	
37. Cambridge Washington Academy	Cambridge	Washington	March 20, 1815.	
38. Greenville Academy	Greenville	Greene	February 27, 1816.	
39. St. Lawrence Academy	Potsdam	St. Lawrence	March 25, 1816.	
40. Hartwick Seminary	Hartwick	Otsego	August 13, 1816.	
41. Middlebury Academy	Middlebury	Wyoming	January 26, 1819.	
42. Cortland Academy	Homer	Cortland	February 2, 1819.	
43. Delaware Academy	Delhi	Delaware	February 2, 1820.	
44. Franklin Academy	Prattsburgh	Steuben	February 23, 1824.	
45. Hamilton Academy	Hamilton	Madison	February 23, 1824.	
46. Mount Pleasant Academy	Mount-Pleasant	Westchester	April 3, 1827.	
47. Monroe Academy	Henrietta	Monroe	July 2, 1827.	Extinct.
48. Lewiston High School Academy	Lewiston	Niagara	April 16, 1828.	
49. Owego Academy	Owego	Tioga	April 16, 1828.	
50. Oneida Institute of Science and Industry	Whitesborough.	Oneida	March 24, 1829.	Extinct.

51. Franklin Academy*	Malone	Franklin	April 28, 1831.	
52. Clarkson Academy	Clarkson	Monroe	March 17, 1835.	
53. Amenia Seminary	Amenia	Dutchess	March 29, 1836.	
54. Stillwater Academy	Stillwater	Saratoga	January 29, 1839.	Extinct.
55. Kingsborough Academy	Kingsborough	Fulton	February 5, 1839.	
56. Rochester Collegiate Institute	Rochester	Monroe	February 26, 1839,	Extinct.
57. Munro Academy	Elbridge	Onondaga	April 23, 1839.	
58. Moravia Institute	Moravia	Cayuga	January 23, 1840.	
59. Schuylerville Academy	Schuylerville	Saratoga	January 23, 1840.	
60. Sherburne Union Academy	Sherburne	Chenango	January 23, 1840.	
61. Union Village Academy	Union-Village	Washington	January 23, 1840.	
62. Phipps Union Seminary	Albion	Orleans	February 11, 1840.	
63. Herkimer County Academy	Herkimer	Herkimer	February 11, 1840.	
64. Elmira Academy	Elmira	Chemung	March 31, 1840.	Extinct.
65. Le Roy Female Seminary	Le Roy	Genesee	February 16, 1841.	Extinct.
66. Moriah Academy	Moriah	Essex	February 16, 1841.	
67. Rhinebeck Academy	Rhinebeck	Dutchess	February 23, 1841.	
68. Argyle Academy	Argyle	Washington	May 4, 1841.	
69. Gilbertsville Academy and Collegiate Institute	Gilbertsville	Otsego	May 4, 1841.	
70. Jordan Academy	Jordan	Onondaga	January 12, 1842.	
71. Glens Falls Academy	Glens Falls	Warren	January 12, 1842.	
72. Brockport Collegiate Institute	Brockport	Monroe	February 15, 1842.	
73. Clinton Seminary	Clinton	Oneida	February 15, 1842.	Extinct.
74. Augusta Academy	Augusta	Oneida	February 28, 1842.	
75. Piermont Academy	Piermont	Rockland	March 15, 1842.	
76. De Lancey Institute	Hampton	Oneida	April 13, 1842.	Extinct.
77. Binghamton Academy	Binghamton	Broome	August 23, 1842.	
78. Yates Academy	Yates Centre	Orleans	August 23, 1842.	
79. Champlain Academy	Champlain	Clinton	August 23, 1842.	
80. Alfred Academy	Alfred	Allegany	January 31, 1843.	
81. Cortlandville Academy	Cortlandville	Cortland	January 31, 1843.	
82. Perry-Centre Institute	Perry-Centre	Wyoming	January 31, 1843.	
83. Monroe Academy	Henrietta	Monroe	February 7, 1843.	

* No. 51. **Franklin Academy, (Malone) charter made perpetual, June 23, 1851.**

CATALOGUE OF ACADEMIES.—(CONTINUED.)

NAMES.	Town.	County.	Date of incorporation.	Remarks.
84. Norwich Academy	Norwich	Chenango	February 14, 1843.	
85. Ball Seminary	Hoosick Falls	Rensselaer	April 11, 1843.	
86. Astoria Institute	Newtown	Queens	February 13, 1844.	
87. New Berlin Academy	New Berlin	Chenango	February 13, 1844.	
88. Chester Academy	Chester	Orange	February 27, 1844.	
89. The Academy at Little Falls	Little Falls	Herkimer	October 17, 1844.	
90. Nunda Literary Institute	Nunda	Livingston	January 30, 1845.	
91. Rensselaerville Academy	Rensselaerville	Albany	January 30, 1845.	
92. Whitestown Seminary	Whitestown	Oneida	March 27, 1845.	
93. Genesee and Wyoming Seminary	Alexander	Genesee	March 27, 1845.	
94. Cary Collegiate Seminary	Caryville	Genesee	May 16, 1845.	
95. New Paltz Academy	New Paltz	Ulster	October 11, 1845.	
96. Galway Academy	Galway	Saratoga	October 11, 1845.	
97. Lancaster Academy	Lancaster	Erie	January 22. 1846.	
98. Sand Lake Academy	Sandlake	Rensselaer	February 19, 1846.	
99. Wilson Collegiate Institute	Wilson	Niagara	February 19, 1846.	
100. Riga Academy	Riga	Monroe	May 11, 1846.	
101. Genoa Academy	Genoa	Cayuga	February 4, 1847.	
102. Brookfield Academy	Brookfield	Madison	April 17, 1847.	
103. De Ruyter Institute	De Ruyter	Madison	December 3, 1847.	
104. Sag Harbor Institute	Sag Harbor	Suffolk	January 20, 1848.	
105. Starkey Seminary	Starkey	Yates	February 25, 1848.	
106. Stillwater Seminary	Stillwater	Saratoga	February 25, 1848.	
107. Whitehall Academy	Whitehall	Washington	October 27, 1848.	
108. Addison Academy	Addison	Steuben	February 8, 1849.	
109. Friendship Academy	Friendship	Allegany	February 8, 1849.	
110. Windsor Academy	Windsor	Broome	March 15, 1849.	
111. Sauquoit Academy	Sauquoit	Oneida	April 6, 1849.	
112. Brownville Female Seminary	Brownville	Jefferson	January 10, 1850.	

No.	Academy	Location	County	Date	Remarks
113.	Prattsville Academy	Prattsville	Greene	January 31, 1850.	
114.	Hubbardsville Academy	Hubbard'sCor's	Madison	February 14, 1850.	
115.	Holley Academy	Holley	Orleans	March 28, 1850.	
116.	Richburgh Academy	Richburgh	Allegany	April 12, 1850.	
117.	New-York Conference Seminary	Charlotteville	Schoharie	October 26, 1850.	
118.	Randolph Academy Association	Randolph	Cattaraugus	January 24, 1851.	
119.	Prospect Academy	Prospect	Oneida	January 24, 1851.	
120.	Half-Moon Academy	Half Moon	Saratoga	February 14, 1851.	
121.	West Winfield Academy	West Winfield	Herkimer	February 14, 1851.	
122.	Buffalo Female Academy	Buffalo	Erie	October 14, 1851.	
123.	Orleans Academy	Orleans	Jefferson	February 5, 1851.	
124.	Rushford Academy	Rushford	Allegany	March 4, 1852.	
125.	Unadilla Academy	Unadilla	Otsego	April 1, 1852.	
126.	Monticello Academy†	Monticello	Sullivan	April 1, 1852.	
127.	Rural Academy	Montgomery	Orange	April 1, 1852.	
128.	Peterboro' Academy	Peterboro'	Madison	January 28, 1853.	
129.	Rogersville Union Seminary	Rogersville	Steuben	January 28, 1853.	
130.	Ellington Academy	Ellington	Chautauque	February 11, 1853.	
131.	Yates Polytechnic Institute	Chittenango	Madison	April 11, 1853.	
132.	Olean Academy‡	Olean	Cattaraugus	June 3, 1853.	
133.	Grammar School of Madison University	Hamilton	Madison	June 17, 1853.	Under act of April 17, 1838.
134.	Carlisle Seminary†	Carlisle	Schoharie	October 20, 1853.	
135.	Princetown Academy†	Princetown	Schenectady	October 20, 1853.	
136.	Fort Plain Seminary and Female Collegiate Inst†	Fort Plain	Montgomery	October 20, 1853.	
137.	Elmira Collegiate Seminary†	Elmira	Chemung	October 20, 1853.	

† Provisional Charters.

‡ This Academy was incorporated April 11, 1853, under the name of "Olean Academy Association." The charter was amended, and present name granted June 3, 1853.

Of these 137 Academies,

2, Hamilton Oneida Academy, and Geneva Academy, have been merged in Colleges; Hamilton College and Geneva (now Hobart Free) College

16 Are extinct: Union Academy, at Stone Arabia; Otsego Academy, at Cooperstown; Columbia Academy, at Kinderhook; Catskill Academy, Newburgh Academy, Ballston Academy, Washington Academy, at Warwick; Blooming-grove Academy, Monroe Academy, Oneida Institute of Science and Industry, at Whitesborough; Stillwater Academy, Clinton Seminary, Rochester Collegiate Institute, Elmira Academy, Le Roy Female Seminary and De Lancey Institute.

1. Stillwater Academy was reincorporated under the name of Stillwater Seminary. Le Roy Female Seminary is now Ingham Collegiate Institute in the next catalogue.

118 Remaining, subject to the visitation of the Regents.

IV. CATALOGUE OF ACADEMIES

And similar institutions of Learning, incorporated by the Legislature, made up to January 1, 1854, with the date of their incorporation, and the period when any of them was received under the visitation of the Regents of the University.

NAMES.	Town.	County.	Date of incorporation.	Time when they became subject to the Regents.
1. Clinton Grammar School	Clinton	Oneida	March 28, 1817.	February 27, 1826.
2. New-York Institution for Deaf and Dumb	New-York	New-York	April 15, 1817.	Act of April 15, 1830.
3. Waterford Female Academy	Waterford	Saratoga	March 19, 1819.	
4. Mount Pleasant Academy	Mount Pleasant	Westchester	March 24, 1820.	
5. Catskill Female Seminary	Catskill	Greene	March 24, 1820.	
6. Albany Female Academy	Albany	Albany	February 16, 1821.	January 29, 1828.
7. Newtown Female Academy	Newtown	Queens	March 15, 1822.	
8. Cooperstown Female Academy	Cooperstown	Otsego	April 15, 1822.	
9. Ithaca Academy	Ithaca	Tompkins	March 24, 1823.	Act of April 17, 1826.
10. Redhook Academy	Red Hook	Dutchess	April 23, 1823.	February 23, 1829.
11. Kinderhook Academy	Kinderhook	Columbia	April 3, 1824.	February 19, 1828.
12. Fredonia Academy	Fredonia	Chautauque	November 25, 1824.	February 23, 1830.
13. Jefferson Academy	Jefferson	Schoharie	November 27, 1824.	January 22, 1833.
14. Seminary of the Genesee Conference*	Cazenovia	Madison	April 6, 1825.	January 29, 1828.
15. Ontario Female Seminary	Canandaigua	Ontario	April 14, 1825.	January 29, 1828.
16. Bridgewater Academy	Bridgewater	Oneida	April 8, 1826.	April 16, 1828.
17. Bedford Academy	Bedford	Westchester	April 8, 1826.	
18. Rye Academy	Rye	Westchester	April 13, 1826.	
19. Canajoharie Academy	Canajoharie	Montgomery	April 13, 1826.	February 26, 1828.
20. Rensselaer Oswego Academy†	Mexico	Oswego	April 13, 1826.	January 4, 1833.
21. Ovid Academy	Ovid	Seneca	April 13, 1826.	January 26, 1830.
22. New-Rochelle Academy	New-Rochelle	Westchester	April 13, 1826.	
23. Union Literary Society	Bellville	Jefferson	April 13, 1826.	January 5, 1830.
24. Steuben Academy	Steuben	Oneida	April 17, 1826.	January 29, 1828.
25. Scientific and Military Academy of Western Dist.	Whitesborough	Oneida	April 17, 1826.	January 9, 1829.

No.	Name	Place	County	Month	Day, Year	Remarks
26.	Livingston County High School‡	Geneseo	Livingston	March	10, 1827.	February 7, 1829.
27.	Rochester High School§	Rochester	Monroe	March	15, 1827.	April 19, 1831.
28.	Springville Academy.	Springville	Erie	March	19, 1827.	January 26, 1830.
29.	Gaines Academy	Gaines	Orleans	April	14, 1827.	January 26, 1830.
30.	Buffalo High School Association‖	Buffalo	Erie	April	17, 1827.	
31.	Flushing Institute	Flushing	Queens	April	16, 1827.	
32.	Granville Academy	Granville	Washington	March	31, 1828.	April 16, 1830.
33.	Gouverneur High School¶	Gouverneur	St. Lawrence	April	5, 1828.	February 19, 1829.
34.	Sullivan County Academy	Bloomingburgh	Sullivan	April	5, 1828.	March 31, 1831.
35.	Albany Female Seminary	Albany	Albany	April	9, 1828.	April 16, 1828.
36.	Yates County Academy and Female Seminary	Penn-Yan	Yates	April	17, 1828.	January 25, 1830.
37.	Cortland Female Seminary	Homer	Cortland	April	18, 1828.	
38.	Rochester Institute of General Education	Rochester	Monroe	April	19, 1828.	
39.	White Plains Academy	White-Plains	Westchester	April	19, 1828.	January 26, 1830.
40.	Plattsburgh Academy	Plattsburgh	Clinton	April	21, 1828.	March 4, 1829.
41.	Harlaem Literary and Scientific Academy	New-York	New-York	January	24, 1829.	
42.	Palmyra High School	Palmyra	Wayne	March	28, 1829.	July 2, 1833.
43.	Skaneateles Academy	Skaneateles	Onondaga	April	14, 1829.	
44.	Brooklyn C. Institute for Young Ladies	Brooklyn	Kings	April	23, 1829.	
45.	Ontario High School	Victor	Ontario	April	6, 1830.	
46.	Highland-Grove Gymnasium	Fishkill	Dutchess	April	11, 1831.	
47.	Fort Covington Academy	Fort-Covington	Franklin	April	21, 1831.	See act of April 21, 1831.
48.	Buffalo Female Seminary	Buffalo	Erie	April	23, 1831.	
49	Claverack Academy	Claverack	Columbia	April	25, 1831.	February 5, 1839.
50	Greenbush and Schodack Academy	Greenbush	Rensselaer	April	25, 1831.	February 27, 1841.
51.	Genesee Manual Labor Seminary	Bethany	Genesee	April	13, 1832.	See also act of March 27, 1834
52.	Rochester Inst. of Practical Education	Rochester	Monroe	April	14, 1832.	
53.	Bernville Academy and Female Seminary	Bern	Albany	March	8, 1833.	

* No. 14. **Name altered** (March 24, 1829) to Seminary of Genesee and Oneida Conference, and again (May 8, 1835) to ***Oneida Conference Seminary.***
† No. 20. Name altered (May 14, 1845) to Mexico Academy.
‡ No. 26. **Name altered** (act of May 13, 1846) to Geneseo Academy.
§ No. 27. Merged in Rochester Collegiate Institute.
‖ No. 30. Name altered to Buffalo Literary and Scientific Academy. Dissolved by act of the Legislature April 21, 1846.
¶ No. 33. Name altered (April 24, 1840) to Gouverneur Wesleyan Seminary.

CATALOGUE OF ACADEMIES.—(CONTINUED.)

NAMES.	Town.	County.	Date of incorporation.	Time when they became subject to the Regents.
54. New-Paltz Academy	New-Paltz	Ulster	April 12, 1833.	April 29, 1836.
55. Oswego Academy	West-Oswego	Oswego	April 25, 1833.	
56. Aurora Manual Labor Seminary*	Aurora	Erie	April 30, 1833.	January 29, 1839.
57. Genesee and Wesleyan Seminary†	Lima	Livingston	April 30, 1833.	Act of March 9, 1836.
58. Oswegatchie Academy	Oswegatchie	St. Lawrence	April 26, 1833.	
59. Poughkeepsie Female Seminary	Poughkeepsie	Dutchess	March 19, 1834.	
60. Mayville Academy	Mayville	Chautauque	April 24, 1834.	February 5, 1839.
61. Holland Patent Academy	Trenton	Oneida	April 24, 1834.	
62. Preble High School	Preble	Cortland	April 24, 1834.	
63. Clermont Academy	Clermont	Columbia	April 26, 1834.	February 26, 1839.
64. Waterford Academy	Waterford	Saratoga	April 28, 1834.	February 5, 1839.
65. Clinton Liberal Institute	Clinton	Oneida	April 29, 1834.	March 29, 1836.
66. Essex County Academy	Westport	Essex	May 1, 1834.	March 6, 1838.
67. New-Woodstock Academy	Cazenovia	Madison	May 2, 1834.	
68. Troy Academy‡	Troy	Rensselaer	May 5, 1834.	February 5, 1839.
69. Alexander Classical School	Alexander	Genesee	May 6, 1834.	February 5, 1839.
70. Manlius Academy	Manlius	Onondaga	April 13, 1835.	January 29, 1839.
71. Delaware Literary Institute	Franklin	Delaware	April 23, 1835.	January 29, 1839.
72. Saratoga Academy and Scientific Institute	Saratoga Spr'gs	Saratoga	April 28, 1835.	
73. Rome Academy§	Rome	Oneida	April 28, 1835.	
74. Syracuse Academy	Syracuse	Onondaga	April 28, 1835.	February 5, 1839.
75. Watertown Academy	Watertown	Jefferson	May 2, 1835.	Ch. rep'ld Feb. 19, 1841.
76. Keeseville Academy	Keeseville	Essex	May 4, 1835.	February 5, 1839.
77. Dover Academy	Dover	Dutchess	May 9, 1835.	
78. Genesee Seminary	Batavia	Genesee	May 11, 1835.	
79. Fishkill Education Society	Fishkill	Dutchess	May 11, 1835.	
80. Nassau Academy	Nassau	Rensselaer	May 11, 1835.	
81. Ogdensburgh Academy	Ogdensburgh	St. Lawrence	April 20, 1835.	February 5, 1839.

No.	Name	Location	County	Incorporated		Admitted
82.	De Ruyter Institute	De Ruyter	Madison	March	30, 1836.	January 30, 1838.
83.	Jamestown Academy	Jamestown	Chautauque	April	16, 1836.	February 5, 1839.
84.	Mendon Academy	Mendon	Monroe	April	20, 1836.	February 5, 1839.
85.	Albany Pearl-street Academy	Albany	Albany	April	23, 1836.	
86.	La Fayette High School	La Fayette	Onondaga	April	23, 1836.	
87.	Avon Academy	Avon	Livingston	April	30, 1836.	February 27, 1841.
88.	Hempstead Seminary	Hempstead	Queens	May	2, 1836.	January 29, 1839.
89.	Schaghticoke Seminary	Schaghticoke	Rensselaer	May	4, 1836.	
90.	Poughkeepsie Female Academy	Poughkeepsie	Dutchess	May	10, 1836,	February 28, 1837.
91.	Mt. Pleasant Female Seminary	Sing-Sing	Westchester	May	10, 1836.	
92.	Angelica Academy	Angelica	Alegany	May	12, 1836.	
93.	Victory Academy	Victory	Cayuga	May	21, 1836.	
94.	Fulton Female Seminary‖	Fulton	Oswego	May	24, 1836.	February 5, 1839.
95.	Black River Literary and Scientific Institute¶	Watertown	Jefferson	May	25, 1836.	January 30, 1838.
96.	Poughkeepsie Collegiate School	Poughkeepsie	Dutchess	May	26, 1836.	February 5, 1839.
97.	Galway Academy	Galway	Saratoga	May	26, 1836.	January 29, 1839.
98.	Norwich Union Seminary	Norwich	Chenango	March	16, 1837.	
99.	Schenectady Young Ladies' Seminary	Schenectady	Schenectady	March	22, 1837.	February 5, 1839.
100.	Schenectady Lyceum and Academy**	Schenectady	Schenectady	March	22, 1837.	February 5, 1839.
101.	Lyons Academy	Lyons	Wayne	March	29, 1837.	
102.	Southold Academy	Southold	Suffolk	April	21, 1837.	
103.	Rochester Female Academy	Rochester	Monroe	April	21, 1837.	February 5, 1839.
104.	Ames Academy	Ames	Montgomery	April	22, 1837.	February 5, 1839.
105.	Canton Academy	Canton	St. Lawrence	April	24, 1837.	January 23, 1840.
106.	Seneca Falls Academy	Seneca Falls	Seneca	April	27, 1837.	February 5, 1839.
107.	Schoharie Academy	Schoharie	Schoharie	April	28, 1837.	February 5, 1839.
108.	Utica Female Academy	Utica	Oneida	April	28, 1837.	February 5, 1839.

* No. 56. Name altered (act of April 16, 1838) to Aurora Academy.

† No. 57. New act of incorporation, (May 1, 1834) and styled Genesee Wesleyan Seminary.

‡ No. 68. See also act passed May 8, 1837.

§ No. 73. Act revised and amended January 28, 1848. See No. 161.

‖ No. 94. Name altered (April 11, 1842) to Fulton Academy; and again (April 11, 1849) to "The Falley Seminary of the Black River Conference."

¶ No. 95. Name altered (act of May 12, 1846) to Jefferson County Institute.

** No. 100. Schenectady Lyceum and Academy is allowed to educate females, by act passed March 28, 1839.

CATALOGUE OF ACADEMIES.—(CONTINUED.)

NAMES.	Town.	County.	Date of incorporation.	Time when they became subject to the Regents.
109. Albion Acade y	Albion	Orleans	May 1, 1837.	February 27, 1841.
110. Dunkirk Academy	Dunkirk	Chautauque	May 1, 1837.	
111. Collinsville Institute	West-Turin	Lewis	May 2, 1837.	
112. Fayetteville Academy	Fayetteville	Onondaga	May 4, 1837.	February 5, 1839.
113. Coxsackie Academy	Coxsackie	Greene	May 5, 1837.	February 5, 1839.
114. Westfield Academy	Westfield	Chautauque	May 5, 1837.	February 5, 1839.
115. Troy Female Seminary	Troy	Rensselaer	May 6, 1837.	January 30, 1838.
116. Groton Academy	Groton	Tompkins	May 6, 1837.	January 29, 1839.
117. Knoxville Academy	Knox	Albany	May 9, 1837.	February 15, 1842.
118. Hudson River Agricultural Seminary	Stockport	Columbia	May 16, 1837.	
119. Windsor Academy	Windsor	Broome	May 16, 1837.	
120. Batavia Female Academy	Batavia	Genesee	March 5, 1838.	February 5, 1839.
121. Pembroke and Darien Classical School	Pemb'ke, Darien	Genesee	April 6, 1838.	
122. East Bloomfield School	East-Bloomfield	Ontario	April 9, 1838.	January 23, 1840.
123. Rutgers Female Institute	New-York	New-York	April 10, 1838.	January 23, 1840.
124. Peekskill Academy	Peekskill	Westchester	April 16, 1838.	February 5, 1839.
125. Vernon Academy	Vernon	Oneida	April 18, 1838.	February 5, 1839.
126. Auburn Female Seminary	Auburn	Cayuga	April 18, 1838.	February 11, 1840.
127. Weedsport Academy	Weedsport	Cayuga	April 18, 1838.	
128. Hobart-Hall Institute	Holland Patent	Oneida	March 11, 1839.	January 23, 1840.
129. Marion Academy	Marion	Wayne	March 27, 1839.	
130. Literary and Scientific Institute of York	York	Livingston	March 27, 1839.	
131. Red Creek Union Academy	Red Creek	Wayne	March 27, 1839.	February 5, 1846.
132. Amsterdam Female Seminary	Amsterdam	Montgomery	March 29, 1839.	February 16, 1841.
133. Seward Female Seminary of Rochester	Rochester	Monroe	April 5, 1839.	February 11, 1840.
134. Royalton Centre Academy	Royalton	Niagara	April 9, 1839.	
135. Troy Episcopal Institute	Troy	Rensselaer	April 13, 1839.	
136. Westtown Academy	West-Town	Orange	April 18, 1839.	January 30, 1840.

137. Whitehall Academy	Whitehall	Washington	April	20, 1839.	
138. Turin Academy	Turin	Lewis	April	30, 1839.	
139. Ridgebury Academy	Minisink	Orange	April	30, 1839.	February 11, 1840.
140. Broome Academy	Union	Broome	April	30, 1839.	
141. Wallabout Select Grammar School of the 7th ward in the city of Brooklyn	Brooklyn	Kings	May	4, 1839.	
142. Millville Academy	Millville	Orleans	April	25, 1840.	February 16, 1841.
143. Lyons Academy*	Lyons	Wayne	May	7, 1840.	
144. The Proprietors of St Paul's College	Flushing	Queens	May	9, 1840.	
145. Bethany Academy	Bethany	Genesee	March	29, 1841.	February 28, 1842.
146. Walworth Academy	Walworth	Wayne	May	12, 1841.	April 19, 1843.
147. Lockport Academy	Lockport	Niagara	May	26, 1841.	
148. Walkill Academy	Walkill	Orange	May	26, 1341.	February 13, 1842.
149. Macedon Academy	Macedon	Wayne	April	11, 1842.	January 30, 1845.
150. Palmyra Academy	Palmyra	Wayne	April	11, 1842.	
151. Waterloo Academy	Waterloo	Seneca	April	11, 1842.	August 23, 1842.
152. Grammar School of Columbia College	New-York	New-York			By act of April 17, 1838.
153. Grammar School of the University of the city of New, York	New-York	New-York			By act of April 17, 1838.
154. Eastern Collegiate Institute of the city of New-York	New York	New-York	May	7, 1844.	
155. Brooklyn Female Academy	Brooklyn	Kings	May	8, 1845.	January 14, 1847.
156. Spencertown Academy	Spencertown	Rensselaer	May	13, 1845.	December 3, 1847.
157. Fonda Academy	Fonda	Montgomery	May	13, 1845.	October 11 1845.
158. Rensselaer Institute	Troy	Rensselaer	May	8, 1837.	February 5, 1846.
159. New-York Free Academy	New-York	New-York	May	7, 1847.	October 31, 1849.
160. S. S. Seward Institute	Fonda	Orange	May	7, 1847.	February 4, 1848.
161. Rome Academy	Rome	Oneida	January	28, 1848.	March 15, 1849.
162. Clover-street Seminary	Brighton	Monroe	April	7, 1848.	February 23, 1849.
163. Mansion Square Female Seminary	Poughkeepsie	Dutchess	March	15, 1849.	
164. Liberty Normal Institute	Liberty	Sullivan	April	10, 1849.	September 20, 1849.
165. Academy of the Sacred Heart	Rochester	Monroe	April	11, 1849.	

CATALOGUE OF ACADEMIES.—(Continued.)

NAMES.	Town.	County.	Date of Incorporation.	Time when they became subject to the Regents.
166. Lockport Union School	Lockport	Niagara	March 18, 1850.	October 26, 1850.
167. Jonesville Academy	Clifton Park	Saratoga	April 1, 1850.	October 26, 1850.
168. Medina Academy	Medina	Orleans	April 10, 1850.	April 25, 1851.
169. Female Academy of the Sacred Heart	New-York	New-York	July 9, 1851.	
170. Collegiate Institute of the city of New-York	New-York	New-York	July 10, 1851.	
171. Ingham Collegiate Institute	Le Roy	Genesee	April 6, 1852.	January 28, 1853.
172. Packer Collegiate Institute	Brooklyn	Kings	March 19, 1853.	
173. Geneva Union School	Geneva	Ontario	April 15, 1853.	
174. Utica Academy	Utica	Oneida	May 26, 1853.	
175. Pulaski Academy	Pulaski	Oswego	June 4, 1853.	
176. Auburn Female Seminary ?	Auburn	Cayuga	January 29, 1852. and July 21, 1853.	

103 Of the Academies incorporated by the Legislature, including the institution for the instruction of the Deaf and Dumb at New-York, the Grammar School of Columbia College, and the Grammar School of the University of the city of New-York, 176 in number, one hundred and three have been received under the visitation of the Regents.

But of these,

18 Bridgewater Academy, Scientific and Military Academy of the Western District, Rochester High School, Gaines Academy, White Plains Academy, Fort Covington Academy, Waterford Academy, Alexander Classical School, Syracuse Academy, Poughkeepsie Classical School, Batavia Female Academy, Auburn Female Seminary, Seward Female Seminary, Palmyra High School, New Paltz Academy, Galway Academy, Waterloo Academy and Brooklyn Female Academy, have either become extinct, or their property is otherwise transferred.

85 Remaining subject to the visitation of the Regents.

* No. 143. By referring to No. 101, it will be seen that an Academy under that name (Lyons Academy) was incorporated March 29, 1837.

V. CATALOGUE

OF ACADEMIES UNDER THE VISITATION OF THE REGENTS.

(Arranged according to counties.)

1. ALBANY:
   1. Albany Academy,
   2. Albany Female Academy,
   3. Albany Female Seminary,
   4. Knoxville Academy,
   5. Rensselaerville Academy, ... 5

2. ALLEGANY:
   1. Alfred Academy,
   2. Friendship Academy,
   3. Richburgh Acedemy,
   4. Rushford Academy, ... 4

3. BROOME:
   1. Binghamton Academy,
   2. Windsor Academy,......................... 2

4. CATTARAUGUS:
   1. Olean Academy,
   2. Randolph Academy Association, ... 2

5. CAYUGA:
   1. Auburn Academy,
   2. Cayuga Academy,
   3. Genoa Academy,
   4. Moravia Institute,........................ 4

6. CHAUTAUQUE:
   1. Ellington Academy,
   2. Fredonia Academy,
   3. Jamestown Academy,
   4. Mayville Academy,
   5. Westfield Academy,...................... 5

7. Chemung:

1. Elmira Collegiate Seminary,................ 1

8. Chenango:

1. New Berlin Academy,
2. Norwich Academy,
3. Oxford Academy,
4. Sherburne Union Academy, ... 4

9. Clinton:

1. Champlain Academy,
2. Plattsburgh Academy, ... 2

10. Columbia:

1. Claverack Academy,
2. Clermont Academy,
3. Hudson Academy,
4. Kinderhook Academy,
5. Spencertown Academy, ... 5

11. Cortland:

1. Cortland Academy,
2. Cortlandville Academy,.................... 2

12. Delaware:

1. Delaware Academy,
2. Delaware Literary Institute, ... 2

13. Dutchess:

1. Amenia Seminary,
2. Dutchess County Academy,
3. Poughkeepsie Female Academy,
4. Redhook Academy,
5. Rhinebeck Academy,...................... 5

14. Erie:

1. Aurora Academy,
2. Buffalo Female Academy,
3. Lancaster Academy,
4. Springville Academy, ... 4

15. Essex:

1. Essex County Academy,
2. Keeseville Academy,
3. Moriah Academy,........................ 3

16. Franklin:

1. Franklin (Malone) Academy,............... 1

17. Fulton:

1. Johnstown Academy,
2. Kingsborough Academy,.................... 2

18. Genesee:

1. Bethany Academy,
2. Cary Collegiate Institute,
3. Genesee and Wyoming Seminary,
4. Ingham Collegiate Institute,................ 4

19. Greene:

1. Coxsackie Academy,
2. Greenville Academy,
3. Prattsville Academy,...................... 3

20. Hamilton: (None.)

21. Herkimer:

1. Academy at Little Falls,
2. Fairfield Academy,
3. Herkimer Academy,
4. West Winfield Academy,................... 4

22. Jefferson:

1. Brownville Female Seminary,
2. Jefferson County Institute,
3. Orleans Academy,
4. Union Literary Society, ... 4

23. Kings:

1. Erasmus Hall,....... 1

24. Lewis :

1. Lowville Academy, ... 1

25. Livingston :

1. Avon Academy,
2. Genesee Wesleyan Seminary,
3. Geneseo Academy,
4. Nunda Literary Institute, ... 4

26. Madison :

1. Brookfield Academy,
2. De Ruyter Institute,
3. Hamilton Academy,
4. Hubbardsville Academy,
5. Grammar School of Madison University,
6. Oneida Conference Seminary,
7. Peterboro' Academy,
8. Yates Polytechnic Institute, ... 8

27. Monroe :

1. Brockport Collegiate Institute,
2. Clarkson Academy,
3. Clover-street Seminary,
4. Mendon Academy,
5. Monroe Academy,
6. Riga Academy,
7. Rochester Female Academy,................ 7

28. Montgomery :

1. Ames Academy,
2. Amsterdam Female Seminary,
3. Canajoharie Academy,
4. Fonda Academy,
5. Fort Plain Sem. & Female Collegiate Institute, 5

29. New-York :

1. Deaf and Dumb Institution, New-York,
2. Grammar School of Columbia College,
3. Grammar School of University of city of New-York,
4. New-York Free Academy,
5. Rutgers' Female Institute,.................. 5

30. NIAGARA:

1. Lewiston Academy,
2. Lockport Union School,
3. Wilson Collegiate Institute,.................. 3

31. ONEIDA:

1. Augusta Academy,
2. Clinton Grammar School,
3. Clinton Liberal Institute,
4. Hobart Hall Institute,
5. Prospect Academy,
6. Rome Academy,
7. Sauquoit Academy,
8. Steuben Academy,
9. Utica Academy,
10. Utica Female Academy,
11. Vernon Academy,
12. Whitesborough Academy,
13. Whitestown Seminary,...................... 13

32. ONONDAGA:

1. Fayetteville Academy,
2. Jordan Academy,
3. Manlius Academy,
4. Munro Academy,
5. Onondaga Academy,
6. Pompey Academy,.......................... 6

33. ONTARIO:

1. Canandaigua Academy,
2. East Bloomfield Academy,
3. Ontario Female Seminary,.................. 3

34. ORANGE:

1. Chester Academy,
2. Farmers' Hall,
3. Montgomery Academy,
4. Ridgebury Academy,
5. Rural Academy,
6. S. S. Seward Institute,
7. Walkill Academy,
8. Westtown Academy, ... 8

35. Orleans:

1. Albion Academy,
2. Holley Academy,
3. Medina Academy,
4. Millville Academy,
5. Phipps Union Seminary,
6. Yates Academy, ... 6

36. Oswego:

1. Falley Seminary,
2. Mexico Academy,........................ 2

37. Otsego:

1. Cherry Valley Academy,
2. Gilbertsville Academy and Collegiate Institute,
3. Hartwick Seminary,
4. Unadilla Academy,........................ 4

38. Putnam: (None.)

39. Queens:

1. Astoria Institute,
2. Hempstead Seminary,
3. Oysterbay Academy,
4. Union Hall,........................ 4

40. Rensselaer:

1. Ball Seminary,
2. Greenbush and Schodack Academy,
3. Lansingburgh Academy,
4. Rensselaer Institute,
5. Sandlake Academy,
6. Troy Academy,
7. Troy Female Seminary, ... 7

41. Richmond: (None.)

42. Rockland:

1. Piermont Academy, ... 1

43. St. Lawrence :

1. Canton Academy,
2. Gouverneur Wesleyan Seminary,
3. Ogdensburgh Academy,
4. St. Lawrence Academy,.................... 4

44. Saratoga :

1. Galway Academy,
2. Half-Moon Academy,
3. Jonesville Academy,
4. Schuylerville Academy,
5. Stillwater Seminary,.............. 5

45. Schenectady :

1. Princetown Academy,
2. Schenectady Academy,
3. Schenectady Lyceum and Academy,
4. Schenectady Young Ladies' Seminary,........ 4

46. Schoharie :

1. Carlisle Seminary,
2. Jefferson Academy,
3. New-York Conference Seminary,
4. Schoharie Academy,....................... 4

47. Seneca :

1. Ovid Academy,
2. Seneca Falls Academy, ... 2

48. Steuben :

1. Addison Academy,
5. Franklin Academy, (Prattsburgh,)
3. Rogersville Union Seminary,................ 3

49. Suffolk :

1. Clinton Academy,
2. Sag Harbor Institute,...... 2

50. SULLIVAN :

1. Liberty Normal Institute,
2. Monticello Academy,
3. Sullivan County Academy, ... 3

51. TIOGA :

1. Owego Academy, ... 1

52. TOMPKINS :

1. Groton Academy,
2. Ithaca Academy, ... 2

53. ULSTER :

1. Kingston Academy,
2. New-Paltz Academy, ... 2

54. WARREN :

1. Glen's Falls Academy, ... 1

55. WASHINGTON :

1. Argyle Academy,
2. Cambridge Washington Academy,
3. Granville Academy,
4. Union Village Academy,
5. Washington Academy,
6. Whitehall Academy, ... 6

56. WAYNE :

1. Macedon Academy,
2. Red Creek Union Academy,
3. Walworth Academy, ... 3

57. WESTCHESTER :

1. Mount Pleasant Academy,
2. North Salem Academy,
3. Peekskill Academy, ... 3

58. Wyoming :

1. Middlebury Academy,
2. Perry Centre Institute,.................. ... 2

59. Yates :

1. Starkey Seminary,
2. Yates Co. Academy and Female Seminary,.... 2

205

VI. CATALOGUE

OF INDIVIDUALS ON WHOM THE HONORARY DEGREE OF DOCTOR OF LAWS HAS BEEN CONFERRED BY THE REGENTS OF THE UNIVERSITY.

Years.	
1792,............	Robert R. Livingston.
1792,............	William Patterson.
1829,............	William A. Duer.
1834,............	Benjamin F. Butler.
1844,............	William L. Marcy.
1849,............	Alexander H. Stevens.
1849,............	Harvey P. Peet.
1849,............	Salem Town.
1850,............	Joseph Henry.
1851,............	Valentine Mott.

VII. CATALOGUE

OF THE REGENTS OF THE UNIVERSITY OF THE STATE OF NEW-YORK, FROM THE ESTABLISHMENT OF THE UNIVERSITY.

GOVERNORS OF THE STATE, *ex officio*.

Date of election or appointment.	NAMES.	Exitus.
1787.	*George Clinton,	1795
1795.	*John Jay,	1801
1801.	*George Clinton,	1804
1804.	*Morgan Lewis,	1807
1807.	*Daniel D. Tompkins,	1817
1817.	*De Witt Clinton,	1822
1823.	*Joseph C. Yates,	1824
1825.	*De Witt Clinton,	1828
1829.	Martin Van Buren,	1830
1831.	Enos T. Throop,	1832
1833.	William L. Marcy,	1838
1839.	William H. Seward,	1842
1843.	William C. Bouck,	1844
1845.	*Silas Wright,	1846
1847.	*John Young,	1848
1849.	Hamilton Fish,	1850
1851.	Washington Hunt,	1852
1853.	Horatio Seymour,	

LIEUTENANT GOVERNORS, *ex officio*.

1787.	*Pierre Van Cortlandt,	1795
1795.	*Stephen Van Rensselaer,	1801
1801.	*Jeremiah Van Rensselaer,	1804
1804.	*John Broome,	1812
1812.	*De Witt Clinton,	1814

* Deceased.

Date of election or appointment.	NAMES.	Exitus
1814.	*John Tayler, ...	1822
1823.	*Erastus Root,............	1824
1825.	*James Talmadge, ...	1826
1827.	*Nathaniel Pitcher,........................	1828
1829.	Enos T. Throop, ...	1830
1831.	*Edward P. Livingston,..	1832
1833.	John Tracy,................................	1838
1839.	Luther Bradish, ...	1842
1843.	Daniel S. Dickinson, ...	1844
1845.	Addison Gardiner, ...	1847
1847.	Hamilton Fish,.............................	1848
1849.	George W. Patterson,.......................	1850
1851.	Sanford E. Church, ...	

SECRETARIES OF STATE, *ex officio*.**

1842.	*Samuel Young, ...	1845
1845.	Nathaniel S. Benton, ...	1847
1848.	Christopher Morgan, ...	1851
1852.	Henry S. Randall.	

REGENTS.

Date of election or appointment.	NAMES.	Exitus.
1787, Apr. 13.	*Rev. John Rogers, D. D., ... died	1811
1787, Apr. 13.	*Egbert Benson, LL. D., ... resigned	1802
1787, Apr. 13.	*Gen. Philip Schuyler, ... died	1804
1787, Apr. 13.	*Ezra L'Hommedieu, ...died	1811?
1787, Apr. 13.	*Rev. Nathan Kerr, ...died	1804?
1787, Apr. 13.	*Peter Sylvester, ... died	1808?
1787, Apr. 13.	*John Jay, LL. D., ... resigned	1790
1787, Apr. 13.	*Rev. Dirck Romeyn, D. D., ...resigned	1796
1787, Apr. 13.	*James Livingston, ...resigned	1797
1787, Apr. 13.	*Ebenezer Russel, ...resigned	1813
1787, Apr. 13.	*Lewis Morris, ...died	1798?
1787, Apr. 13.	*Matthew Clarkson, ...died	1825

* Deceased.

** By virtue of an act passed April 8, 1842.

Date of election or appointment.	NAMES.		Exitus.
1787, Apr. 13.	*Right Rev. Benj. Moore, D. D.,	resigned	1792
1787, Apr. 13.	*Rev. Eliardus Westerlo, D. D.,	died	1790
1787, Apr. 13.	*Rev. Andrew King,	died	1815
1787, Apr. 13.	*Rev. William Linn, D. D.,	died	1808
1787, Apr. 13.	*Jonathan G. Tompkins,	resigned	1808
1787, Apr. 13.	*Rev. John McDonald,	resigned	1796
1787, Apr. 13.	*Frederic Wm. Baron De Steuben,	died	1794
1790, Mar. 30.	*Gulian Verplanck,	died	1800
1791, Jan. 15.	*Zephaniah Platt,	died	1807
1795, Jan. 28.	*James Watson,	died	1806
1796, Feb. 18.	*James Cochran,	resigned	1819
1797, Jan. 11.	*Abraham Van Vechten, LL. D.,	resigned	1823
1797, Feb. 28.	*Rev. Thomas Ellison,	died	1802
1798, Mar. 13.	*Simeon De Witt,	died	1834
1800, Feb. 3.	*James Kent, LL. D.,	vacated	1816
1802, Feb. 1.	*John Tayler,	died	1829
1802, Feb. 15.	*Henry Rutgers,	resigned	1826
1802, Feb. 18.	*Charles Selden,	vacated	1816
1805, Jan. 28.	*Ambrose Spencer, LL. D.,	vacated	1816
1805, Jan. 28.	*Lucas Elmendorf,	vacated	1822
1807, Feb. 11.	*Elisha Jenkins,	died	1848
1808, Feb. 14.	*De Witt Clinton, LL. D.,	resigned	1825
1808, Feb. 14.	*Peter Gansevoort,	died	1812
1808, Feb. 14.	*Alexander Sheldon,	vacated	1816
1809, Jan. 31.	*Nathan Smith,	vacated	1822
1812, Feb. 28.	*Joseph C. Yates,	vacated	1833
1812, Feb. 28.	*Solomon Southwick,	resigned	1823
1813, Mar. 3.	*Smith Thompson, LL. D.,	resigned	1819
1813, Mar. 3.	*John Woodworth, LL. D.,	resigned	1822
1816, Mar. 4.	Martin Van Buren, LL. D.,	resigned	1829
1817, Jan. 28.	*John Lansing, Jun., LL. D.	died	1828
1817, Jan. 28.	*Rev. John De Witt, D. D.,	resigned	1823
1817, Jan. 28.	*Samuel Young,	resigned	1835
1819, Jan. 28.	*Nathan Williams,	vacated	1824
1819, Mar. 16.	*Stephen Van Rensselaer, LL. D.,	died	1839
1820, Feb. 1.	William A. Duer, LL. D.,	vacated	1824
1822, Feb. 7.	*James Thompson,	died	1845

* Deceased.

Date of election or appointment.	NAMES.	Exitus.
1822, Feb. 7.	*Harmanus Bleecker, LL. D.,...resigned	1834
1823, Feb. 14.	*Samuel A. Talcott, ...resigned	1829
1823, Feb. 14,	*James King, ...died	1841
1823, Feb. 14.	*Peter Wendell, M, D.,............died	1849
1823, Apr. 9.	William L. Marcy, LL. D.,. ....vacated	1829
1824, Feb. 13.	*Peter B. Porter, ...resigned	1830
1824, Feb. 13.	*Robert Troup,...............resigned	1827
1825, Jan. 12.	John Greig, ...	
1826, Jan. 26.	*Jesse Buel, ...died	1839
1826, Jan. 26.	Gulian C. Verplanck, LL. D, ...	
1827, Feb. 20.	*Edward P. Livingston, ...resigned	1831
1829, Feb. 29.	Benjamin F. Butler, LL. D.,,..resigned	1832
1829, Mar. 31.	Gerrit Y. Lansing, ...	
1829, Mar. 31.	John K. Paige, ...	
1827, Mar. 31.	*John Suydam, ...died	1835
1830, Apr. 2.	*John P. Cushman, ...resigned	1834
1830, Apr. 2.	John Tracy, ...resigned	1833
1831, Mar. 23.	John A. Dix, LL. D., ... resigned	1846
1832, Feb. 6.	*John L. Viele, ...died	1832
1833, Feb. 5.	*William Campbell, ...died	1844
1833, Feb. 5.	Erastus Corning,.....................	
1833, Apr. 4.	Prosper M. Wetmore,.................	
1834, Apr. 17.	*James McKown, ...died	1847
1833, Apr. 17.	John Lorimer Graham, ...	
1835, Jan. 20.	Amasa J. Parker, ... resigned	1844
1835, Apr. 8.	John McLean,.........................	
1835, May 9.	Washington Irving, LL. D., ...resigned	1842
1839, Feb. 18,	*Joseph Russell,.............. resigned	1844
1840, Feb. 28.	John C. Spencer, LL. D., ...vacated	1844
1842, Feb. 1.	Gideon Hawléy, LL. D., ...	
1842, Mar. 24.	David Buel,..........................	
1844, May 4.	James S. Wadsworth,..................	
1844, May 4.	John V. L. Pruyn, ...	
1845, Feb. 3.	William C. Bouck,............vacated	1847

*Deceased.

Date of election or appointment.	NAMES.	Exitus.
1845, Feb. 3.	Martin Van Buren, LL. D.,....resigned	1845
1845, May 10.	Jabez D. Hammond. LL. D.,..........	
1846, Feb. 2.	John L. O'Sullivan,.................	
1846, Feb. 2.	Robert Campbell,...................	
1847, May 6.	Rev. Samuel Luckey, D. D..,.........	
1847, Sep. 22.	Robert G. Rankin,..................	
1849, Feb. 6.	Philip S. Van Rensselaer,............	
1851, Mar. 18.	Rev. John N. Campbell, D. D.,........	

OFFICERS OF THE BOARD OF REGENTS.

CHANCELLORS OF THE UNIVERSITY.

Date of appointment.		Exitus.
1787, July 17.	George Clinton,	1796
1796, Jan. 20.	John Jay,	1802
1802, Feb. 15.	George Clinton,	1805
1805, Feb. 4.	Morgan Lewis,	1808
1808, Feb. 8.	Daniel D. Tompkins,	1817
1817, Feb. 3.	John Tayler,	1829
1829, Mar. 24.	Simeon De Witt,	1834
1835, Jan. 8.	Stephen Van Rensselaer,	1839
1839, Feb. 12.	James King,	1841
1842, Jan. 13.	Peter Wendell,	1849
1849, Oct. 31.	John Greig, *declined*,	1849
1849, Oct. 31.	Gerrit Y. Lansing,	

VICE-CHANCELLORS.

1787, July 17.	John Jay,	1790
1790, Mar. 31.	John Rogers, D. D.,	1808
1808, Feb. 8.	John Rogers, D. D., (re-appointed).	1811
1814, Mar. 14.	John Tayler,	1817
1817, Feb. 3.	Simeon De Witt,	1829
1829, Mar. 24.	Elisha Jenkins,	1842
1842, Jan. 13.	Luther Bradish,	1843
1843, Jan. 12.	Daniel S. Dickinson,	1845
1845, Jan. 9.	John Greig,	

SECRETARIES.

1787, July 17.	Richard Harrison, LL.D.,	1790
1790, April 7.	Nathaniel Lawrence,	1794
1794, Jan. 21.	De Witt Clinton, LL.D.,	1797
1797, Jan. 23.	David S. Jones, LL.D.,	1798
1798, Mar. 19.	Francis Bloodgood,	1814
1814, Mar. 25.	Gideon Hawley, LL.D.,	1841
1841, May 25.	T. Romeyn Beck, M.D.,	

FINIS.

www.ingramcontent.com/pod-product-compliance
Lightning Source LLC
LaVergne TN
LVHW021401110826
845150LV00007B/1737

* 9 7 8 1 4 2 5 5 1 2 6 8 2 *